I WANT TO EAT COOKIES

I WANT TO EAT COOKIES

OVER 90 RECIPES TO KEEP YOUR COOKIE JAR STOCKED YEAR-ROUND

Ellen Morrissey
Photography LENNART WEIBULL

Hardie Grant
NORTH AMERICA

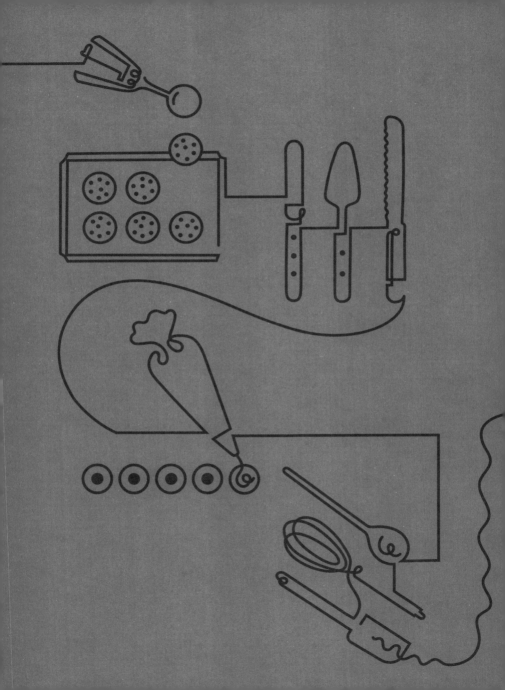

CONTENTS

INTRODUCTION

Chances are, you've heard the expression "easy as pie." If they are so easy, then how come so few home bakers make pies from scratch? Maybe it's because the process is not that simple. The same thing holds true when something effortless is described as, "a piece of cake." Cakes are always appreciated, but they're rarely a breeze to make. You know what is truly easy? Cookies. And they're guaranteed to lift the spirits.

With a few pantry ingredients and some basic equipment, you can bake great cookies from scratch. Lots of them. And with each batch you produce from start to finish, you can begin to build on your experience to create home-baked treats of all sizes, shapes, textures, and flavors. The possibilities are endless, because so many cookie recipes are adaptable. The best ones allow for improvisation, letting you swap out one nut for another or switch a variety of chocolate for your favorite.

The recipes in this collection include dozens of tried and true favorites, many old-fashioned treats and others more of-the-moment delights. Most are put together from recipes I've been baking for years, though I've updated many of them with twists on ingredients or simple shortcuts. In some cases, I've incorporated an alternative flour into a recipe where it does double duty, at once improving the flavor of a cookie and delivering a bit of whole-grain goodness (see the Snickerdoodles on page 30 for an example of subs like these).

My hope is that you'll give each of these recipes a try, and enjoy baking, eating, and sharing cookies of your own for years to come.

BAKING PANTRY ESSENTIALS

To build out your baking larder begin by seeking out the best ingredients you can find; the most frequently used ones are listed on these pages. Whenever possible, opt for those with minimal processing or additives—unbleached flour, for example, and unsalted butter.

1. Flour, including all-purpose and whole wheat
2. Granulated sugar
3. Confectioners' sugar
4. Brown sugar, including light and dark
5. Baking powder
6. Nuts, including walnuts, almonds, pecans, cashews, peanuts
7. Honey
8. Golden syrup
9. Molasses
10. Baking soda
11. Butter
12. Coarse salt
13. Unsweetened cocoa powder
14. Heavy cream
15. Sprinkles, nonpareils, and other decorations
16. Eggs
17. Chocolate, such as bittersweet, semisweet, and milk varieties
18. Extracts, including vanilla and almond
19. Spices, including cinnamon, cardamom, ginger, allspice, and cloves

TOOLS AND EQUIPMENT

For the most consistent and reliable results, it's worth investing in high-quality tools and equipment—sturdy baking sheets, graduated metal measuring cups and spoons, a well-made electric mixer, and so on. Well-made kitchen gear will also last longer than flimsier options.

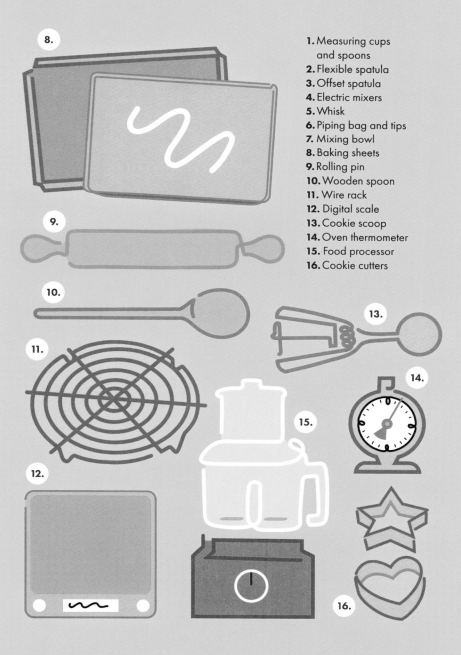

1. Measuring cups and spoons
2. Flexible spatula
3. Offset spatula
4. Electric mixers
5. Whisk
6. Piping bag and tips
7. Mixing bowl
8. Baking sheets
9. Rolling pin
10. Wooden spoon
11. Wire rack
12. Digital scale
13. Cookie scoop
14. Oven thermometer
15. Food processor
16. Cookie cutters

8.

9.

10.

11.

12.

13.

14.

15.

16.

TIPS AND TECHNIQUES FOR MAKING COOKIES

Baking is part science, part art form (in that order). As such, heeding a few suggestions and best practices will serve you well as you bake your way through the recipes in this book.

READ THE RECIPE COMPLETELY before you begin, to avoid realizing halfway through that you don't have enough of everything you need (including time).

RELY ON A STAND-ALONE OVEN THERMOMETER. Not all ovens are calibrated properly, especially older models, and nothing will compromise your success more than baking at the wrong temperature. About 20 minutes before you begin to bake, preheat the oven to the recommended temperature.

USE THE CENTER OVEN RACK if you're only baking one sheet of cookies at a time. For two sheets, situate the racks so that they divide the oven into thirds, and rotate the sheets halfway through the recommended bake time.

BE MINDFUL OF VISUAL CLUES—golden brown on the edges, for example—or other indicators (smell or touch, say) given in the recipe beyond the suggested cooking times.

TO MEASURE LIQUID INGREDIENTS like milk, cream, and water, pour them into clear measuring cups with pour spouts and marked lines to read at eye level. Never use a liquid measuring cup for dry ingredients.

TO MEASURE FLOUR, run a whisk through it, then use the scoop and level method: Spoon the flour into a dry measuring cup until it forms a pile above the rim, then sweep off the excess with a straight-edged spatula. There's no need to sift flour before measuring unless a recipe specifies so.

TO MEASURE SUGAR, first break up any clumps, then dip the cup or spoon straight into the sugar, and level with a straight edge. Light and brown sugars should be firmly packed into dry measuring cups. Confectioners' sugar can be lumpy, so it's best to sift before measuring.

SIFT OR WHISK COCOA POWDER before measuring to remove any clumps.

WIRE RACKS allow for air circulation around cookies as they cool, which helps them stay crisp and dry, not soggy.

COOL BAKING SHEETS completely before you move onto the next batch of cookies.

ALLOW SUFFICIENT TIME for icings and glazes to dry. If cookies are finished with confectioners' sugar or cocoa, wait until just before serving to dust them.

LET COOKIES COOL completely before storing. Keeping cookies in airtight tins, layered between baking parchment or waxed paper, prolongs their freshness.

TO FREEZE STURDY COOKIES, pack them in layers in resealable bags, with baking parchment between each layer. Thaw at room temperature.

EGGS are easiest to separate when they're cold, but best mixed at room temperature. If egg whites will be whisked into a meringue, keep any bits of yolk out of the bowl (the fat in the yolks will inhibit the process). Break the whites into a separate bowl before you add them to the others for your meringue.

TO TOAST NUTS, spread them in an even layer on a rimmed baking sheet, then place in a preheated 350°F (180°C) oven. Toast until fragrant, 8 to 10 minutes depending on the nut, tossing halfway through.

WHEN NUTS ARE CHOPPED, pay attention to how they are measured. If it says, "1 cup (130 g) almonds, chopped," measure the whole nuts first, then chop. The reverse is true for "1 cup (120 g) chopped almonds": chop, then measure.

CHOP CHOCOLATE using a chef's or serrated knife with a long blade, pressing down to make neat chunks for your cookie dough.

TO MELT CHOPPED CHOCOLATE, use a microwave or a small bowl set over (not in) a pan of simmering water. For either method, remove the bowl from the heat at regular intervals and give it a good stir. The last bits should melt from the residual heat.

FRESHLY GROUND SPICES make the best-tasting cookies. Grind whole spices like nutmeg, cardamom, and peppercorns whenever possible, in an electric spice grinder or with a mortar and pestle.

LINING SHEETS WITH BAKING PARCHMENT is easier and more reliable than coating a pan with butter or oil, and allows for the fastest cleanup. Depending on the recipe, you can often flip the parchment over and use the other side a few more times, minimizing waste.

TO CHOP DRIED FRUIT AND CANDIED GINGER, use kitchen shears; if the blades get sticky, dab them with a drop of cooking oil.

TO ZEST CITRUS FRUITS, use a microplane grater; which also works well for fresh ginger.

TO ROLL OUT COOKIE DOUGH for cutting, sandwich it between lightly floured sheets of baking parchment. Cut out cookies as close as possible with lightly floured cutters; use a pastry brush to remove excess flour. Chill the dough after cutting it to maintain sharp edges on your baked cookies.

TO FORM LOGS OF COOKIE DOUGH for chilling, use a paper towel tube with a slit cut down its length. Wrap the log in plastic wrap, then shape it into a cylinder using the split tube. (If the dough is soft, chill for 30 minutes before shaping.) When slicing the chilled logs, use a sharp knife, turning the log as you work to keep the rounds even.

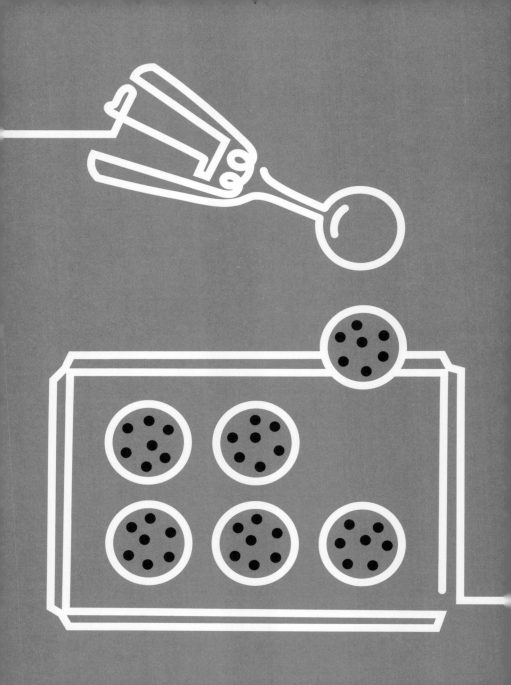

SCOOPED AND
DROPPED

CRISPY CHOCOLATE CHIP COOKIES

MAKES: ABOUT 36
PREP: 10 MINS
CHILL: 0 MINS
BAKE: ABOUT 15 MINS

With the perfect crunch and maximum dunkability, this irresistible version of everyone's favorite cookie has buttery, chocolatey notes in every bite.

INGREDIENTS

1¾ cups plus 2 tablespoons (240 g) all-purpose flour

1¼ teaspoons baking soda

1 teaspoon coarse salt

1 cup (225 g) unsalted butter, at room temperature

1 cup (200 g) granulated sugar

½ cup (110 g) packed brown sugar (dark or light)

2 teaspoons vanilla extract

1 large egg

1¾ cups (335 g) chocolate chips or chunks

1. Preheat the oven to 375°F (190°C) and line two large baking sheets with baking parchment.

2. In a large bowl, whisk together the flour, baking soda, and salt. In a separate bowl, with an electric mixer, beat the butter with both sugars until pale and fluffy. Mix in the vanilla and egg until combined. With the mixer on low speed, gradually add the flour mixture and beat in until just combined. Fold in the chocolate chips.

3. Drop mounds of dough (1½ tablespoons each) onto the sheets, spacing about 2 inches (5 cm) apart. Bake until golden brown and set, 14 to 16 minutes, rotating the sheets halfway through. Transfer the sheets to a wire rack and let the cookies cool for 2 to 3 minutes on the sheets before transferring them directly to the wire rack to cool completely.

CHEWY CHOCOLATE CHIP COOKIES

MAKES : ABOUT 40

PREP : 10 MINS

CHILL : 1 HR

BAKE : 10 MINS

Tender and toothsome, these cookies get their texture from a good dose of brown sugar, two whole eggs, and a little chill time in the refrigerator before baking.

INGREDIENTS

2⅔ cups (335 g) all-purpose flour

1 teaspoon baking soda

¾ teaspoon coarse salt

1 cup (225 g) unsalted butter, at room temperature

1 cup (220 g) packed brown sugar (light or dark)

½ cup (100 g) granulated sugar

2 large eggs

1 teaspoon vanilla extract

2 cups (350 g) semisweet chocolate chips

1. In a large bowl, whisk together the flour, baking soda, and salt. In another bowl, with an electric mixer on medium speed, beat the butter until very soft and creamy. Add both sugars and beat until incorporated. Mix in the eggs and vanilla until well blended. With the mixer on low speed, gradually add the flour mixture and beat in until just combined. Stir in the chocolate chips. Cover and chill the dough until firm, at least 1 hour.

2. Preheat the oven to 375°F (190°C) and line two large baking sheets with baking parchment.

3. Scoop the dough and roll into 1-inch (2.5 cm) balls. Place the balls on the sheets, spacing at least 2 inches (5 cm) apart. Bake until browned on the edges but still soft in the middle, about 10 minutes, rotating the sheets halfway through. Transfer the cookies to wire racks to cool completely.

ANYTHING GOES OATMEAL COOKIES

MAKES: 24
PREP: 10 MINS
CHILL: 0 MINS
BAKE: 15 MINS

Why stop at raisins when considering options for mix-ins? Try swapping in any combination of chocolate chips, nuts, seeds, diced candied ginger, dried fruit, or cocoa nibs instead.

INGREDIENTS

1½ cups (125 g) rolled oats

¼ cup plus 1 tablespoon (60 g) all-purpose flour

¼ cup plus 1 tablespoon (60 g) whole wheat flour

¼ cup (30 g) toasted wheat germ

½ teaspoon baking soda

½ teaspoon baking powder

¼ teaspoon coarse salt

½ cup (115 g) unsalted butter, at room temperature

½ cup (100 g) granulated sugar

½ cup (120 g) packed dark brown sugar

1 large egg

½ teaspoon vanilla extract

¾ to 1 cup (100 to 140 g) mix-ins (see intro above)

1. Preheat the oven to 350°F (180°C) and line two large baking sheets with baking parchment.

2. In a large bowl, whisk together the oats, both flours, wheat germ, baking soda, baking powder, and salt. In another bowl, with an electric mixer, beat the butter and both sugars together until pale and creamy. Mix in the egg and vanilla until combined. On low speed, add the flour mixture, then your choice of mix-ins.

3. Using a mini-scoop or level tablespoon, form the dough into balls and place on the baking sheets, spacing about 2 inches (5 cm) apart.

4. Bake until golden brown on the edges, 12 to 15 minutes (on the longer side if you like them crisp), rotating the baking sheets halfway through. Transfer the sheets to a wire rack and let the cookies cool for 5 minutes on the sheets before transferring them to the wire rack to cool completely.

SCOOPED AND DROPPED

VANILLA WAFERS

MAKES : ABOUT 50

PREP : 10 MINS

CHILL : 0 MINS

BAKE : 12 MINS

INGREDIENTS

2½ cups (325 g) all-purpose flour

1½ teaspoons baking powder

1 teaspoon coarse salt

1 cup (225 g) unsalted butter, at room temperature

1⅓ cups (260 g) sugar

2 large eggs

2 tablespoons vanilla extract

2 tablespoons milk or water

It may seem futile to try to bake a vanilla wafer from scratch that rivals the supermarket favorite. This one manages to do just that, with bold vanilla flavor and a nice crunch.

1. Preheat the oven to 375°F (190°C) and line two baking sheets with baking parchment.

2. In a bowl, whisk together the flour, baking powder, and salt. In another bowl, with an electric mixer on medium speed, beat the butter and sugar until pale and fluffy. Add the eggs and vanilla and beat until combined. With the mixer on low speed, beat in half the flour mixture, then the milk, then the remaining flour mixture.

3. Drop level teaspoons of the dough onto the sheets, spacing 2 inches (5 cm) apart. With damp fingertips, flatten the tops slightly and make sure their shapes are round. Bake until golden brown around the edges, about 12 minutes, rotating the sheets halfway through. Transfer the cookies to a wire rack to cool completely.

BROWN BUTTER AND TOFFEE CHIP COOKIES

MAKES: ABOUT 36

PREP: 15 MINS

CHILL: 1¾ HRS

BAKE: 13 MINS

The marriage of brown butter, toffee, and chocolate is hard to beat, which makes this cookie nearly impossible to resist.

INGREDIENTS

½ cup (115 g) salted butter, cut into tablespoons

2¼ cups (280 g) all-purpose flour

1 teaspoon baking soda

½ teaspoon coarse salt

⅔ cup (140 g) granulated sugar

⅔ cup (140 g) packed brown sugar (light or dark)

2 large eggs

2 teaspoons vanilla extract

⅔ cup (90 g) toffee bar bits (such as Heath)

⅔ cup (105 g) milk chocolate chips

1. In a saucepan over medium heat, melt the butter until boiling. Cook, swirling the pan frequently and watching closely, until it has a nutty fragrance and the flecks on the bottom of the pan are deep brown, about 6 minutes. Pour the butter into a heatproof bowl, scraping out the browned bits, and chill until just firm, about 45 minutes.

2. In a large bowl, whisk together the flour, baking soda, and salt. In another bowl, with an electric mixer, beat the butter with both sugars until creamy. Beat in the eggs and vanilla until smooth. On low speed, gradually add the flour mixture, scraping down the bowl. Stir in the toffee and chocolate chips. Chill the dough until firm, 1 hour.

3. Preheat the oven to 350°F (180°C) and line two large baking sheets with baking parchment. Drop level tablespoons of dough onto the sheets, spacing 1½ inches (4 cm) apart. Bake until lightly golden, about 13 minutes, rotating the sheets halfway through. Let the cookies cool on the sheets for 3 minutes, then transfer to wire racks to cool completely.

SNICKERDOODLES

MAKES: ABOUT 48
PREP: 10 MINS
CHILL: 1 HR
BAKE: 13 MINS

A couple of twists—namely, swapping in whole grain flour for some of the all-purpose, and adding cardamom to the spice mixture — take this bake sale classic over the top.

INGREDIENTS

2 cups (250 g) all-purpose flour

¾ cup (105 g) whole wheat flour (or light rye)

1½ teaspoons cream of tartar

1 teaspoon baking soda

1 teaspoon coarse salt

1 cup (225 g) unsalted butter, room temperature

1½ cups (300 g) granulated sugar

2 large eggs

¾ cup (150 g) demerara (raw) sugar

1½ teaspoons ground cinnamon

1½ teaspoons ground cardamom (preferably freshly ground)

1. In a large bowl, whisk together both flours, the cream of tartar, baking soda, and salt.

2. In another large bowl, with an electric mixer, beat the butter and granulated sugar until light and fluffy. Mix in the eggs and beat just until combined. On low speed, gradually add the flour mixture until incorporated. Cover and chill the dough until firm, about 1 hour.

3. Preheat the oven to 350°F (180°C). Line two large baking sheets with baking parchment.

4. In a small bowl, whisk together the demerara sugar, cinnamon, and cardamom.

5. Form level tablespoons of the dough into balls, then roll them in the spiced-sugar mixture to coat completely. Place the balls on the baking sheets, spacing 2 inches (5 cm) apart and flattening each lightly with the bottom of a measuring cup or your fingertips. Bake until the cookies are light golden on the edges, about 13 minutes, rotating the baking sheets halfway through. Take care not to overbake. Transfer the cookies to wire racks to cool completely.

TRIPLE-THREAT GINGERSNAPS

MAKES : ABOUT 48

PREP : 10 MINS

CHILL : 15 MINS

BAKE : 15 MINS

INGREDIENTS

2 tablespoons finely grated fresh ginger

½ cup (100 g) granulated sugar, plus extra for rolling

2½ cups (315 g) all-purpose flour

1 cup (130 g) whole wheat flour

1 tablespoon ground ginger

2 teaspoons ground cinnamon

1 teaspoon ground cloves

¼ teaspoon each ground cardamom, coriander, black pepper, and nutmeg

1 teaspoon coarse salt

2 teaspoons baking soda

2 teaspoons boiling water

1 cup (225 g) unsalted butter, at room temperature

⅓ cup (85 g) packed dark brown sugar

½ cup (170 g) molasses

½ cup (65 g) finely chopped candied ginger

Too much ginger? No such thing. Studded with freshly grated, ground, and candied ginger, these snaps make the case that more of this flavorful root is indeed more.

1. In a food processor, combine the fresh ginger and granulated sugar, and pulse to make a paste. In a large bowl, whisk together both flours with the spices and salt. In a small bowl, combine the baking soda with the water.

2. With an electric mixer, beat the butter with the brown sugar until creamy. Beat in the ginger paste, followed by the baking soda mixture and the molasses. On low speed, add the flour mixture until combined. Fold in the candied ginger.

3. Preheat the oven to 350°F (180°C) and line two large baking sheets with baking parchment. Chill the dough while the oven heats.

4. Place some extra sugar for rolling on a large plate. Using a mini-scoop or level tablespoon, form the dough into balls and roll in the sugar to coat completely. Transfer to the sheets, spacing 2 inches (5 cm) apart. Bake until the cookies are set and cracks have formed in their tops, 12 to 15 minutes, rotating the sheets halfway through. Transfer the sheets to wire racks and let the cookies cool on the sheets for 3 minutes before transferring to the racks to cool completely.

BUTTERSCOTCH BLONDIE COOKIES

MAKES: ABOUT 48

PREP: 10 MINS

CHILL: 1 HR

BAKE: 12 MINS

Here's an easy, fuss-free treat to tuck into lunchboxes or add to a holiday cookie tray. Enjoy leftovers sandwiched with ice cream.

INGREDIENTS

1 cup (225 g) unsalted butter, melted and cooled slightly

1 cup (220 g) packed dark (or light) brown sugar

1 cup (200 g) granulated sugar

1 teaspoon coarse salt

2 large eggs

2 teaspoons vanilla extract

2 cups (250 g) all-purpose flour

1 cup (185 g) butterscotch chips

1½ cups (165 g) toasted walnuts or pecans, broken into pieces or coarsely chopped

1. Combine the butter, both sugars, and salt together in a large bowl (you can do this by hand or with an electric mixer). Mix in the eggs and vanilla. Add the flour, stirring to incorporate, then fold in the butterscotch chips and nuts. Chill the dough until firm, about 1 hour.

2. Preheat the oven to 375°F (190°C). Line two large baking sheets with baking parchment.

3. Using a small cookie scoop or tablespoon, drop the dough onto the sheets, spacing 2 inches (5 cm) apart. Bake until golden brown and crisp on the edges, 10 to 12 minutes, rotating the sheets halfway through. Transfer the sheets to a wire rack and let the cookies cool for 5 minutes. Transfer the cookies to the racks to cool.

SALTED CASHEW CRISPS

MAKES : ABOUT 36
PREP : 10 MINS
CHILL : 0 MINS
BAKE : 10 MINS

Ground cashews help create a dough that's wonderfully rich and flavorful, with half the amount of butter of similar drop cookie recipes.

INGREDIENTS

2 cups (250 g) all-purpose flour

1 teaspoon baking soda

2 cups (240 g) lightly salted cashews, plus about 36 halves for topping

1 cup (200 g) granulated sugar

¼ cup (60 g) unsalted butter, melted

1 cup (220 g) packed dark brown sugar

2 large eggs

¼ cup (60 ml) whole milk

1. Preheat the oven to 375°F (190°C). Line two large baking sheets with baking parchment.

2. In a large bowl, whisk together the flour and baking soda. In a food processor, combine the cashews with ¼ cup (50 g) of the granulated sugar. Pulse the machine until the nuts are just coarsely chopped (not too fine).

3. Using an electric mixer, beat the melted butter with the dark brown sugar, the remaining ¾ cup (150 g) granulated sugar, the eggs, and milk until smooth. Add the flour mixture and chopped cashews and beat until just combined.

4. Using a teaspoon, drop mounds of the dough onto the baking sheets, spacing them a few inches apart, and top each with a cashew half. Bake until the cookies are just beginning to brown, about 10 minutes, rotating the sheets halfway through. Transfer the sheets to wire racks and let the cookies cool on the sheets for 3 minutes, then transfer them directly to the racks to cool completely.

HOT COCOA COOKIES

MAKES: ABOUT 18

PREP: 10 MINS

CHILL: 30 MINS

BAKE: 10 MINS

A cup of hot chocolate is reinvented as a cookie—with milk chocolate chips, mini marshmallows, and a trace of cinnamon.

INGREDIENTS

1 cup (125 g) all-purpose flour

¼ cup plus 2 tablespoons (50 g) unsweetened cocoa powder

½ teaspoon baking soda

¼ teaspoon coarse salt

¼ teaspoon ground cinnamon

½ cup (115 g) unsalted butter, at room temperature

½ cup (100 g) granulated sugar

¼ cup (60 g) packed dark brown sugar

1 large egg

1 teaspoon vanilla extract

¾ cup (120 g) milk chocolate chips

¾ cup (40 g) mini marshmallows or ½ cup (20 g) marshmallow bits

1. In a large bowl, whisk together the flour, cocoa, baking soda, salt, and cinnamon. In another bowl, with an electric mixer, beat the butter with both sugars until creamy. Beat in the egg and vanilla. With the mixer on low speed, beat in the flour mixture. Stir in the chocolate chips and marshmallows by hand. Chill the dough until firm, at least 30 minutes.

2. Preheat the oven to 350°F (180°C) and line two baking sheets with baking parchment.

3. Using a small cookie scoop or tablespoon, form the dough into balls and transfer to the baking sheets, spacing 2 inches (5 cm) apart. Bake until the cookies are crisp around the edges and just starting to set in the center, about 10 minutes, rotating the sheets halfway through. Transfer to a wire rack and let the cookies cool completely.

NUTTY MACAROONS

MAKES : ABOUT 36
PREP : 10 MINS
CHILL : 0 MINS
BAKE : 15 MINS

When you want cookies right away but don't have many ingredients on hand, keep this simple recipe in mind. Pecans are the gold standard, but the recipe works with walnuts and almonds, too.

INGREDIENTS

1 ¼ cups (130 g) pecan pieces, very finely chopped, plus pecan halves for topping

¾ cup (150 g) sugar

2 tablespoons all-purpose flour

½ teaspoon coarse salt

1 large egg white

1 teaspoon vanilla extract

1. Preheat the oven to 300°F (150°C) and line two large baking sheets with baking parchment.

2. In a large bowl, stir together the chopped pecans, sugar, flour, salt, egg white, and vanilla. Roll the dough into 1-inch (2.5 cm) balls and place them on the baking sheets, spacing 1 ½ inches (4 cm) apart. Place a pecan half atop each ball, pressing to flatten.

3. Bake just until set, 15 minutes (or for 5 minutes longer if you prefer a crisper cookie). Transfer the cookies to a wire rack to cool completely.

MILK CHOCOLATE HAZELNUT MERINGUES

MAKES: ABOUT 18
PREP: 15 MINS
CHILL: 0 MINS
BAKE: 18 MINS

INGREDIENTS

1 scant cup (120 g) hazelnuts

2 large egg whites

⅛ teaspoon coarse salt

⅓ cup (65 g) sugar

½ teaspoon vanilla extract

1 teaspoon lemon juice

5 ounces (140 g) milk chocolate, melted and cooled slightly

Nutella lovers (in other words, everyone) will flip for these crisp-on-the-outside, tender-on-the-inside treats. The fact that they are gluten-free only broadens their wide appeal.

1. Preheat the oven to 350°F (180°C) and line two large baking sheets with baking parchment.

2. Place the hazelnuts on a baking sheet and toast in the oven for about 10 minutes, tossing halfway through. Transfer to a clean kitchen towel. Close the towel around the nuts and let them steam for a few minutes before rubbing them around to slough off the skins as much as you can. Let the nuts cool before coarsely chopping them.

3. Using an electric mixer, beat the egg whites and salt on medium-low speed until foamy and just beginning to hold a soft peak. Increase the speed to medium and gradually add the sugar, alternating with the vanilla and lemon juice. When all the sugar has been added, increase the speed to high and beat until the whites hold a stiff peak. Using a flexible spatula, fold in the melted chocolate, leaving some white streaks. Gently fold in the nuts.

4. Using a teaspoon, drop rounded mounds of the mixture onto the sheets, spacing 2 inches (5 cm) apart. Bake until just set on the outside but still soft in the center, 12 to 14 minutes. Transfer the meringues to a wire rack to cool.

FLOURLESS DOUBLE CHOCOLATE COOKIES

MAKES : ABOUT 26
PREP : 10 MINS
CHILL : 0 MINS
BAKE : 12 MINS

If you like intensely chocolatey baked goods, look no further. Try a combination of chopped chocolate (white and dark are pictured) and a little flaky salt on top.

INGREDIENTS

2⅔ cups (290 g) confectioners' sugar

¾ cup (65 g) unsweetened cocoa powder, naturally (not Dutch) processed

½ teaspoon coarse salt

3 large egg whites

1 tablespoon vanilla extract

1¼ cups (225 g) chocolate chips or chopped chocolate

Flaky sea salt, for sprinkling (optional)

1. Preheat the oven to 375°F (190°C) and line two large baking sheets with baking parchment.

2. In a large bowl, whisk together the sugar, cocoa, and salt. In another bowl, whisk the egg whites and vanilla until foamy. Pour the egg white mixture into the dry ingredients and stir until just combined. Fold in the chocolate chips. The dough will be quite sticky.

3. Drop level tablespoons onto the sheets, spacing about 2 inches (5 cm) apart and sprinkling lightly with flaky salt, if using. Bake until the edges of the cookies look firm and the tops are glossy, about 12 minutes, rotating the sheets halfway through. They will continue to set as they cool. Transfer the sheets to wire racks and let the cookies cool for 5 minutes, then transfer them to the racks to cool completely.

GRANOLA COOKIES

MAKES: ABOUT 36
PREP: 10 MINS
CHILL: 0 MINS
BAKE: 16 MINS

This chunky drop cookie is filled with good-for-you grains, and fiber-rich dried fruit. Try it as a grab-and-go breakfast or an afternoon pick-me-up.

INGREDIENTS

½ cup plus 2 tablespoons (95 g) all-purpose flour

½ cup (65 g) whole wheat flour

½ teaspoon baking soda

1 teaspoon coarse salt

½ cup (115 g) unsalted butter, at room temperature

½ cup (120 g) lightly packed dark brown sugar

⅓ cup (65 g) granulated sugar

1 large egg

1 teaspoon vanilla extract

1 cup (120 g) granola of your choice

⅓ cup (40 g) cacao nibs or finely chopped dark chocolate

½ cup (35 g) chopped dried apricots, figs, or dates, or whole dried cherries, or cranberries

1. Preheat the oven to 350°F (180°C) and line two large baking sheets with baking parchment.

2. In a large bowl, whisk together both flours, the baking soda, and salt. In another bowl, with an electric mixer, beat the butter with both sugars until pale and fluffy. Scrape down the sides of the bowl and mix in the egg and vanilla. On low speed, beat in the flour mixture until incorporated. Fold in the granola, nibs, and dried fruit by hand until well combined.

3. Scoop mounds of dough (about 2 tablespoons each), roll into balls, and place on the sheets, spacing 3 inches (7.5 cm) apart. Bake until golden brown at the edges and set, about 16 minutes (longer if you prefer them crisper). Transfer the sheets to a wire rack and let the cookies cool for 5 minutes before transferring them directly to the racks to cool completely.

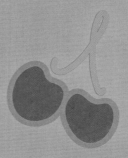

SESAME TAHINI COOKIES

MAKES : ABOUT 36
PREP : 10 MINS
CHILL : 20 MINS
BAKE : 18 MINS

A riff on the peanut butter classic, with sesame paste swapped in and black and white sesame seeds to finish. Try sandwiching a couple of cookies with your favorite jam.

INGREDIENTS

1 ¼ cups plus 2 tablespoons (185 g) all-purpose flour

½ teaspoon baking powder

½ teaspoon baking soda

¼ teaspoon coarse salt

¾ cup (175 g) smooth, well-stirred tahini

½ cup (115 g) unsalted butter, at room temperature

⅓ cup (80 g) packed light brown sugar

⅓ cup (65 g) granulated sugar, plus ¼ cup (50 g) for rolling

1 large egg

1 ½ teaspoons vanilla extract

⅓ cup (45 g) sesame seeds, for rolling (black, white, or a combination of the two)

1. In a mixing bowl, whisk together the flour, baking powder, baking soda, and salt. In another bowl, with an electric mixer, beat the tahini and butter on medium speed until smooth. Add the brown sugar and ⅓ cup (65 g) of the granulated sugar and beat until pale and fluffy. Beat in the egg and vanilla. Reduce the speed to low and gradually add the flour mixture, mixing until combined. Chill the dough until firm, about 20 minutes.

2. Meanwhile, preheat the oven to 350°F (180°C) and line two large baking sheets with baking parchment. In a small bowl, combine the sesame seeds with the remaining ¼ cup (50 g) of the granulated sugar.

3. Form level tablespoons of dough into balls. Roll each ball in the sesame seed mixture, and transfer to the sheets, spacing 2 inches (5 cm) apart. Bake until the cookies are golden on the edges, 16 to 18 minutes. Transfer the sheets to wire racks, and let the cookies cool for 3 minutes before transferring to the racks to cool completely.

CHOCOLATE, OLIVE OIL, AND BUCKWHEAT COOKIES

MAKES : ABOUT 48
PREP : 10 MINS
CHILL : 1¼ HRS
BAKE : 12 MINS

Olive oil makes a fine foundation for a tender cookie; here its nuanced flavor works well with cocoa, buckwheat flour, and cacao nibs.

INGREDIENTS

½ cup (65 g) all-purpose flour

¼ cup (35 g) buckwheat flour

⅓ cup (30 g) unsweetened cocoa powder

½ teaspoon baking soda

¼ teaspoon salt

¼ cup (60 ml) olive oil

1 large egg

¾ cup (150 g) granulated sugar

2 tablespoons honey

1 teaspoon vanilla extract

⅓ cup (40 g) cacao nibs, plus extra for rolling

Demerara (raw) sugar, for rolling

1. In a bowl, whisk both flours, the cocoa, baking soda, and salt. In another bowl, whisk the oil, egg, granulated sugar, honey, and vanilla. Fold the flour mix into the oil mix; fold in the nibs. Chill the dough until firm, 1 hour.

2. Line two large baking sheets with baking parchment. Combine ¼ cup (80 g) each cocoa nibs and demerara sugar in a shallow bowl.

3. Using a level teaspoon, scoop the dough into balls and roll in the sugar mixture to coat. Place on the sheets, spacing 2 inches (5 cm) apart and chill for 15 minutes. Meanwhile, preheat the oven to 350°F (180°C).

4. Bake until the cookies are just set, about 12 minutes, rotating the sheets halfway through. Transfer to a wire rack to cool completely.

TOASTED OAT-PEANUT COOKIES

MAKES : ABOUT 30

PREP : 15 MINS

CHILL : 0 MINS

BAKE : 14 MINS

Toasting the oats in melted butter enhances their nutty flavor. You can use chopped almonds and almond butter in place of the peanuts and peanut butter if you prefer.

INGREDIENTS

¾ cup (170 g) unsalted butter, at room temperature

1 cup (80 g) old-fashioned rolled oats

¾ cup (95 g) all-purpose flour

¼ cup plus 2 tablespoons (70 g) barley flour

1 teaspoon baking soda

¾ teaspoon coarse salt

⅓ cup (65 g) granulated sugar

½ cup (110 g) packed light brown sugar

1 large egg

½ cup (115 g) creamy peanut butter

⅓ cup (45 g) peanuts and ⅓ cup (55 g) milk chocolate chips or ⅔ cup (70 g) chopped lightly salted peanuts

1. Preheat the oven to 350°F (180°C). Line two large baking sheets with baking parchment.

2. In a saucepan, melt ¼ cup (60 g) of the butter over medium-low heat. Add the oats and cook until toasted, stirring occasionally, about 10 minutes. Spread the oats out on a baking sheet and let cool.

3. Meanwhile, in a medium bowl, whisk together both flours, the baking soda, and salt. With an electric mixer, beat the remaining ½ cup (115 g) butter with both sugars until light and fluffy. Add the egg and peanut butter, beating until just combined. On low speed, add the cooled oats, followed by the flour mixture. Stir in the nuts and chocolate chips, if using.

4. Using a tablespoon or mini-scoop, form the dough into balls and place on the sheets, spacing 1 inch (2.5 cm) apart. Bake until the cookies are golden brown, 12 to 14 minutes, rotating the sheets halfway through. Take care not to overbake. Transfer the sheets to wire racks and let the cookies cool for 5 minutes before transferring to the racks to cool completely.

ANZAC BISCUITS WITH GINGER

MAKES: ABOUT 30
PREP: 10 MINS
CHILL: 0 MINS
BAKE: 12 MINS

Named for the Australian and New Zealand Army Corps, these cookies are well loved down under and all over the world. These are flavored with ground and candied ginger.

INGREDIENTS

1 ½ cups (125 g) old-fashioned rolled oats

1 ½ cups (280 g) unsweetened shredded dried coconut

1 ½ cups (290 g) demerara (raw) sugar

1 ½ cups (240 g) all-purpose flour

1 teaspoon ground ginger

1 cup (225 g) unsalted butter, at room temperature

1 tablespoon golden syrup

1 ⅛ teaspoons baking soda

1 tablespoon boiling water

⅓ cup (45 g) finely chopped candied ginger

1. Preheat the oven to 350°F (180°C) and line two large baking sheets with baking parchment.

2. In a large bowl, stir together the oats, coconut, sugar, flour, and ground ginger. In a small saucepan, melt the butter with the syrup. In a small bowl, combine the baking soda with the boiling water. Pour the baking soda mixture into the butter mixture, then pour everything into the flour mixture and stir until well combined. If the dough feels too dry to hold together, add another tablespoon of water. Fold in the candied ginger.

3. Scoop the dough into portions large enough to roll into 1-inch (2.5 cm) balls. Transfer the balls to the baking sheets, spacing about 2 inches (5 cm) apart. Flatten slightly with your palm and bake until the cookies are golden brown and crisp, about 12 minutes, rotating the sheets halfway through. Transfer the cookies to a wire rack to cool completely.

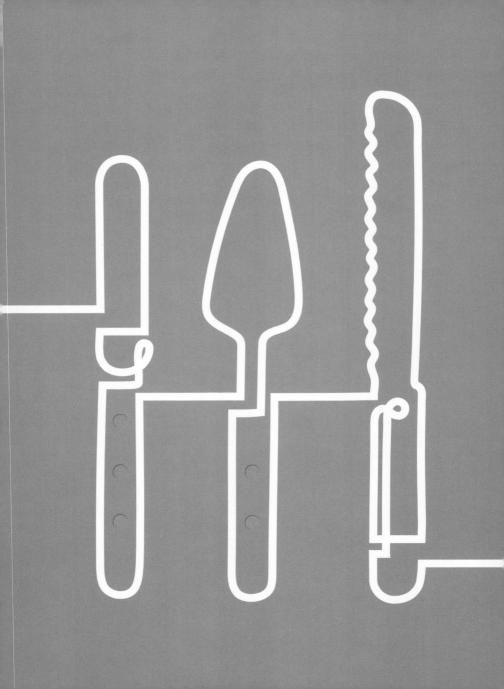

CHILLED AND
SLICED

LEMONY SUGAR COOKIE SLICES

MAKES: ABOUT 24
PREP: 10 MINS
CHILL: 2½ HRS
BAKE: 12 MINS

Nothing fancy here. Just an old-fashioned, beautifully basic, slice-and-bake sugar cookie leveled up with a hearty dose of lemon.

INGREDIENTS

2 cups (250 g) all-purpose flour, plus extra for dusting

½ teaspoon coarse salt

¾ teaspoon baking powder

1 cup (225 g) unsalted butter, at room temperature

1 cup (200 g) granulated sugar

1 packed tablespoon finely grated lemon zest (from 2 to 3 lemons)

2 large egg yolks

1 teaspoon vanilla extract

½ cup (100 g) demerara (raw) sugar, for rolling

1. In a bowl, whisk together the flour, salt, and baking powder. In another bowl, with an electric mixer, beat the butter with the granulated sugar and lemon zest until light and fluffy. Add the egg yolks and vanilla and beat until smooth. With the mixer on low speed, gradually add the flour mixture, beating until just incorporated.

2. On a lightly floured counter (or baking parchment), form the dough into two logs, each 1½ inches (4 cm) in diameter. (If the dough is too soft, chill it for 20 to 30 minutes first.) Wrap each log tightly in plastic wrap, and chill until firm, at least 2 hours.

3. Preheat the oven to 375°F (190°C) and line two large baking sheets with baking parchment. Pour the demerara sugar on a large plate and roll each log in the sugar to coat completely.

4. Slice ¼-inch (5 mm) thick rounds from the logs, and transfer to the sheets, spacing them 1½ inches (4 cm) apart. Bake until just turning golden on the edges, about 12 minutes, rotating the sheets halfway through. Transfer the cookies to a wire rack to cool completely.

CHOCOLATE WAFERS

MAKES: ABOUT 40
PREP: 10 MINS
CHILL: 3 HRS
BAKE: 12 MINS

Thin, crisp, dark chocolatey cookies are often sandwiched with creamy fillings or stacked and layered with whipped cream for an icebox cake (page 176).

INGREDIENTS

1 cup (125 g) all-purpose flour

½ cup (45 g) sifted unsweetened cocoa powder

½ teaspoon baking soda

Rounded ¼ teaspoon coarse salt

¼ teaspoon freshly ground black pepper

6 tablespoons (85 g) unsalted butter, at room temperature

1 cup plus 2 tablespoons (230 g) granulated sugar

1 teaspoon vanilla extract

3 tablespoons water

1. In a large bowl, whisk together the flour, cocoa powder, baking soda, salt, and black pepper. In another bowl, with an electric mixer, beat the butter until very soft. Add the sugar and vanilla and beat in until smooth, then add the water and beat until incorporated. With the mixer on low speed, gradually add the flour mixture and beat until smooth.

2. Form the dough it into a 9-inch (23 cm) log, 1½ inches (4 cm) in diameter. Wrap tightly in plastic wrap, and chill until firm, at least 3 hours.

3. Preheat the oven to 350°F (180°C) and line two large baking sheets with baking parchment.

4. Slice the dough into ¼-inch (5 mm) thick rounds, rotating the logs as needed to keep the shape. Transfer to the prepared sheets, spacing them about 1 inch (2.5 cm) apart. Bake until the cookies are just set and firm, 10 to 12 minutes, rotating the sheets halfway through. Transfer the sheets to wire racks and let the cookies cool completely on the sheets.

WHISKY CURRANT SHORTBREAD

MAKES: ABOUT 48
PREP: 10 MINS
SOAK: 8 HRS
CHILL: 3 HRS
BAKE: 20 MINS

INGREDIENTS

½ cup (120 ml) Scotch whisky

1 cup (130 g) dried currants

2 cups (250 g) all-purpose flour

1 teaspoon coarse salt

½ teaspoon ground ginger

1 cup (225 g) unsalted butter

¾ cup (105 g) confectioners' sugar

1 teaspoon vanilla bean paste or extract

1 teaspoon finely grated orange (or lemon) zest

Demerara (raw) sugar, for rolling

With a generous pour of Scotch used to plump up the currants, these cookies pack a pleasant but not overpowering punch.

1. In a saucepan over medium heat, bring the Scotch whisky and currants to a boil. Transfer to a small bowl, cover, and let soak overnight. Strain the currants through a fine sieve.

2. In a bowl, whisk together the flour, salt, and ginger. In another bowl, with an electric mixer, beat the butter with the sugar, vanilla, and zest until smooth and creamy. With the mixer on low speed, gradually add the flour mixture and beat until incorporated. Fold in the drained currants.

3. Divide the dough in half. Form each half into a log 1½ inches (4 cm) in diameter and wrap tightly in plastic wrap. Chill until firm, at least 3 hours.

4. Preheat the oven to 325°F (160°C) and line two large baking sheets with baking parchment.

5. Place demerara sugar on a large plate; roll the logs in the sugar to coat the outsides completely. Cut the dough into ¼-inch (5 mm) thick slices and transfer to the sheets, spacing 1 inch (2.5 cm) apart. Bake until the cookies are lightly golden, 18 to 20 minutes, rotating the sheets halfway through. Transfer the cookies to wire racks to cool completely.

TOASTED COCONUT SLICES

MAKES: ABOUT 36

PREP: 10 MINS

CHILL: 8½ HRS

BAKE: 15 MINS

Adapted from a recipe by Maida Heatter, this riff includes coconut sugar and almond flour. Drizzled with melted chocolate, they evoke the classic Girl Scouts cookies called Samoas.

INGREDIENTS

1½ cups (185 g) all-purpose flour, plus extra for dusting

½ cup (45 g) almond flour

¾ teaspoon baking powder

½ teaspoon coarse salt

¾ cup (170 g) unsalted butter, at room temperature

½ cup (110 g) packed light brown sugar

½ cup (85 g) coconut sugar

1 teaspoon vanilla extract

⅛ teaspoon almond extract

1 large egg

1¼ cups (95 g) unsweetened shredded coconut, toasted, plus toasted coconut chips for topping (optional)

1. In a large bowl, whisk together both flours, the baking powder, and salt. In another bowl, with an electric mixer, beat the butter with both sugars until pale and fluffy. Mix in the extracts, followed by the egg. With the mixer on low speed, gradually add the flour mixture, beating until just incorporated. Fold in the shredded coconut. Chill the dough until firm, 20 to 30 minutes.

2. On a lightly floured counter, shape the dough into a rectangular log about 2 inches (5 cm) high and 6 inches (15 cm) long. Wrap tightly in plastic wrap and chill overnight.

3. Preheat the oven to 325°F (160°C) and line two large baking sheets with baking parchment.

4. Cut the log into slices, about ¼-inch (5 mm) thick; transfer the slices to the prepared sheets. Top each slice with a couple of coconut chips and bake until the cookies are golden brown and fragrant, about 15 minutes, rotating the sheets halfway through. Transfer the cookies to wire racks to cool completely.

CASHEW AND DARK CHOCOLATE COOKIES

These whole wheat, not-too-sweet, slice-and-bake beauties are just right with a cup of strong espresso or cappuccino.

INGREDIENTS

1 ¼ cups (155 g) whole wheat flour

1 teaspoon baking soda

½ teaspoon coarse salt

½ cup (115 g) unsalted butter, at room temperature

1 cup (200 g) raw sugar

½ cup (130 g) well-stirred cashew or other nut butter

1 large egg, lightly beaten

1 bar (3½ ounces / 100 g) dark chocolate, sliced into flakes

1. In a large bowl, whisk together the flour, baking soda, and salt. In another bowl, with an electric mixer, beat the unsalted butter and sugar together until light and fluffy. Add the cashew butter and beat until blended, then add the egg. With the mixer on low speed, gradually add the flour mixture, beating until just incorporated. Fold in the chocolate flakes.

2. Divide the dough in half and form each into a log, about 6 inches (15 cm) long and 2 inches (5 cm) in diameter. Wrap the log tightly in plastic wrap and chill until firm, at least 3 hours.

3. Preheat the oven to 350°F (180°C) and line two large baking sheets with baking parchment.

4. Cut the logs into ¼-inch (5 mm) thick slices and place the slices on the prepared sheets, spacing them about 1½ inches (4 cm) apart. Bake until set, 12 to 14 minutes, rotating the sheets halfway through. Transfer the sheets to a wire rack to cool for 3 minutes, then transfer the cookies to the rack to cool completely.

PALMIERS

MAKES: ABOUT 48
PREP: 20 MINS
CHILL: 1 HR
BAKE: 11 MINS

Keeping a stash of frozen puff pastry on hand means you can make these three-ingredient wonders (two if you don't count the salt) any time you please.

INGREDIENTS

1¾ cups (350 g) sugar

Large pinch of coarse salt

1 package (about 1 pound / 450 g / 2 sheets) frozen puff pastry, thawed and unfolded

1. Combine the sugar and salt, then pour ¾ cup (150 g) onto a counter. Place a pastry sheet over the sugar and pour another ½ cup (100 g) of the mix over the sheet, all the way to the edges. Roll the sheet until it's ⅛-inch (3 mm) thick and a bit larger all around than 12- by 12-inches (30 by 30 cm), with the sugar pressed into the top and bottom. Trim the edges, then mark the center of the square on one side with a ruler.

2. Working quickly, fold each side in thirds towards the center, leaving ½ inch (1 cm) between each edge and in the center. Close the two sides like a book. You should end up with a tight roll that measures 12 inches (30 cm) long, 2 inches (5 cm) wide, and about half as thick. Wrap tightly in plastic wrap and chill until firm, at least 1 hour. Repeat the process with the second sheet of pastry.

3. Preheat the oven to 425°F (220°C) and line two baking sheets with baking parchment. Slice the dough into ⅜-inch- (1.5 cm) thick slices and place them, cut-sides up, on the sheets. Bake until caramelized and golden on the underside, 6 minutes, then flip over and bake until caramelized on the other side, 4 to 5 minutes. Transfer to wire racks to cool completely.

FRUIT AND NUT OATMEAL ICEBOX COOKIES

MAKES : ABOUT 48
PREP : 10 MINS
CHILL : 3 HRS
BAKE : 12 MINS

Unlike traditional oatmeal cookie recipes, these are formed into logs before baking. Chopping the nuts and fruit very finely makes it easier to slice the chilled dough.

INGREDIENTS

1 cup plus 2 tablespoons (155 g) all-purpose flour

¾ teaspoon coarse salt

1 teaspoon baking soda

1 teaspoon ground ginger

1 cup (225 g) unsalted butter, at room temperature

1 cup plus 2 tablespoons (230 g) granulated sugar

1 cup (240 g) packed dark brown sugar

2 large eggs

1 teaspoon vanilla extract

3 cups (250 g) rolled oats

⅔ cup (80 g) finely chopped dried cranberries

⅔ cup (85 g) finely chopped nuts, such as pecans or walnuts

1. In a large bowl, whisk together the flour, salt, baking soda, and ginger. In another bowl, with an electric mixer, beat the butter with both sugars until pale and creamy. Beat in the eggs one at a time, followed by the vanilla. With the mixer on low speed, add the flour mixture, followed by the oats, cranberries, and nuts, mixing until just incorporated.

2. Divide the dough in half and form each into a log, about 10 inches (25 cm) long and 2 to 3 inches (5 to 7.5 cm) in diameter. (If the dough is too soft to work with, chill it for 20 minutes first.) Wrap each log tightly in plastic wrap and chill until firm, at least 3 hours.

3. Preheat the oven to 350°F (180°C) and line two large baking sheets with baking parchment.

4. Cut one log into ¼-inch (5 mm) thick slices and transfer to the prepared sheets, spacing 2 inches (5 cm) apart. (Keep the other log chilled until ready to bake.)

5. Bake until the cookies are brown all over, about 12 minutes, rotating the sheets halfway through. Transfer the sheets to a wire rack and let cool for 5 minutes, then transfer the cookies to the racks to cool completely.

CORNMEAL FIG BISCOTTI

MAKES: ABOUT 48
PREP: 15 MINS
CHILL: 0 MINS
BAKE: 40 MINS

INGREDIENTS

1½ cups (185 g) all-purpose flour

¾ cup (95 g) stone-ground yellow cornmeal

1 teaspoon baking powder

½ teaspoon fennel seed

Large pinch of coarse salt

3 large eggs, at room temperature

1 cup (200 g) sugar

Finely grated zest of 1 small lemon

¼ teaspoon anise extract or ½ teaspoon vanilla (optional)

1 cup (130 g) walnut halves (or whole almonds), lightly toasted and coarsely chopped

1 heaping cup (150 g) chopped dried figs

Biscotti are not exactly chilled and sliced, but rather baked then sliced then baked again. Nonetheless, they feel at home in this chapter; try almonds in place of the walnuts.

1. Preheat the oven to 350°F (180°C) and line two large baking sheets with baking parchment.

2. In a bowl, whisk the flour, cornmeal, baking powder, fennel, and salt. In a stand mixer, whisk the eggs, sugar, zest, and extract, if using, until pale and thick, 5 minutes. Stir in the flour mixture, then fold in the nuts and figs.

3. Carefully spoon the sticky dough into two long strips on one of the sheets, spacing 3 inches (7.5 cm) apart. With damp hands, form each strip into a 2½-inch (6 cm) wide loaf shape, about 10 inches (25 cm) long. Bake until light golden brown and firm, 25 minutes. Transfer the loaves to a cutting board and cool for 20 minutes. Reduce the oven temperature to 300°F (150°C). With a serrated knife, cut the loaves into ½-inch (1 cm) thick slices and transfer to the sheets, cut-side down. Bake for 15 minutes, then flip over, rotate the sheets, and bake for 10 minutes. Transfer the biscotti to wire racks to cool.

CARAWAY TEA COOKIES

MAKES : ABOUT 24

PREP : 10 MINS

CHILL : 3 HRS 20 MINS

BAKE : 15 MINS

Though it may not look like much, this understated cookie is elegant and refined. Serve with a cup of tea or a glass of bubbly.

INGREDIENTS

2 cups (250 g) sifted all-purpose flour

1 teaspoon baking powder

½ teaspoon ground coriander

½ teaspoon fresh ground black pepper

½ teaspoon ground ginger

¼ teaspoon baking soda

½ teaspoon coarse salt

1 tablespoon caraway seeds, lightly toasted and crushed with the side of a chef's knife

1 cup (225 g) unsalted butter, at room temperature

1 cup (200 g) sugar

1 large egg

1 teaspoon vanilla extract

1. In a large bowl, whisk the flour, baking powder, coriander, pepper, ginger, baking soda, salt, and caraway seeds. In another bowl, with an electric mixer, beat the butter and sugar until light and fluffy. Beat in the egg and vanilla. With the mixer on low speed, gradually add the flour mixture, beating until just incorporated.

2. Chill the dough for 20 minutes, then divide in half and form each half into a log, 9 inches (23 cm) long and 1 ¼ inches (3 cm) in diameter. Wrap tightly in plastic wrap and chill until firm, 3 hours.

3. Cut the logs into ¼-inch (5 mm) thick slices and transfer to the prepared sheets, spacing them 1 ½ inches (4 cm) apart. Chill for 20 minutes.

4. Meanwhile, preheat the oven to 375°F (190°C) and line two large baking sheets with baking parchment. Bake the cookies just until golden around the edges, 12 to 15 minutes, rotating the sheets halfway through. Transfer the cookies to wire racks to cool completely.

SPECULAAS

MAKES : ABOUT 48
PREP : 10 MINS
CHILL : 8 ½ HRS
BAKE : 10 MINS

INGREDIENTS

¾ cup (150 g) demerara (raw) sugar

2 cups (250 g) all-purpose flour

1 tablespoon ground cinnamon

½ teaspoon ground mace

¼ teaspoon ground cardamom

¼ teaspoon ground allspice

⅛ teaspoon ground cloves

Pinch of ground white pepper

1 teaspoon baking soda

1 teaspoon coarse salt

½ cup (115 g) unsalted butter, at room temperature

2½ tablespoons golden syrup or honey

1 large egg

1 teaspoon vanilla paste or extract

The dough for these Belgian spice cookies is traditionally rolled, cut, and stamped with decorative molds. These ones are formed from easy-to-slice logs and "stamped" with a kitchen mallet.

1. Blitz the sugar in a food processor until finely ground to a powder, 30 seconds. Sift the flour, spices, baking soda, and salt into a large bowl. In another bowl, with an electric mixer, beat the butter and blitzed sugar until creamy. Beat in the syrup, egg, and vanilla. With the mixer on low, gradually add the flour mixture, beating until just incorporated.

2. Transfer the dough to a large sheet of plastic wrap and wrap it tightly. Chill for 30 minutes, then form it into a 9-inch (23 cm) log. Wrap again and chill overnight.

3. Line two large baking sheets with baking parchment. Cut the dough into ¼-inch (5 mm) thick slices and place on the sheets, 1 inch (2.5 cm) apart. Press down on each with a lightly floured ridged meat mallet. Chill while you preheat the oven to 375°F (190°C), about 20 minutes.

4. Bake until the cookies are firm and deep golden brown, 10 minutes, rotating the sheets halfway through. Transfer the sheets to wire racks to cool for 5 minutes, then transfer the cookies to the racks to cool completely.

FILLED AND
STUFFED

BRANDY SNAPS

MAKES: ABOUT 24
PREP: 15 MINS
CHILL: 0 MINS
COOK: 12 MINS

The name brandy snap is a misnomer, as the cookies don't always contain the spirit. These are filled with brandy whipped cream, but you can use any of the creams on page 87.

INGREDIENTS

½ cup (115 g) butter, plus extra softened butter for shaping

1 cup (125 g) all-purpose flour, sifted

1 teaspoon ground ginger

Pinch of coarse salt

⅓ cup (110 g) golden syrup

⅔ cup (145 g) packed light brown sugar

Brandy Whipped Cream (page 87), for filling

1. Preheat the oven to 300°F (150°C) and line two large baking sheets with baking parchment. Coat the handle of a wooden spoon or whisk with softened butter.

2. In a bowl, whisk together the flour, ginger, and salt. In a small saucepan, melt the butter with the syrup and sugar over medium-low heat, stirring until the sugar has dissolved and the mixture is smooth. Remove the pan from the heat and quickly stir in the flour mixture until smooth.

3. Drop teaspoons of batter onto the sheets, fitting five or six per sheet and spacing 4 inches (10 cm) apart. Bake until golden brown and lacy, 10 to 12 minutes.

4. Transfer the sheets to a wire rack and let the snaps cool for 1 to 2 minutes. Loosen them with a spatula, then work quickly to wrap each around the greased handle to form a cylinder. If any of the rounds harden before shaping, return to the oven briefly before loosening and shaping. Let set. Transfer to the rack to cool completely.

5. Once cool, use a pastry bag fitted with a ½-inch (1 cm) plain or star-shaped tip to fill each cylinder with the cream.

FOUR WAYS: WHIPPED CREAM

VANILLA

MAKES : ABOUT 2 CUPS (450 G)

PREP : 10 MINS

CHILL : 0 MINS

BAKE : 0 MINS

INGREDIENTS

1 cup (225 g) cold heavy cream

2 tablespoons confectioners' sugar

1 teaspoon vanilla extract

Cookies and cream make an enduring, very popular pair. Use any of the variations below for sandwich cookies or icebox cakes.

Place the cream, sugar, and vanilla in a large bowl, preferably chilled. With an electric mixer (or by hand), whip the ingredients together on medium-high speed until soft to medium-stiff peaks form.

MAPLE

Whip cream as above, placing the cream and 2 teaspoons maple syrup into the chilled bowl to begin and omitting the confectioners' sugar and vanilla.

BRANDY

Whip cream as above, placing the cream, sugar, and 1 tablespoon brandy into the chilled bowl to begin and omitting the vanilla.

LEMON

Whip cream as above, omitting the vanilla, and stopping when soft peaks form. Fold ½ cup (160 g) Lemon Curd (page 173) into the cream.

PEANUT BUTTER BLOSSOM COOKIES

MAKES: 48
PREP: 15 MINS
CHILL: 0 MINS
BAKE: 10 MINS

These two-bite treats are always the first to disappear at a cookie swap, no matter how many other options are on offer.

INGREDIENTS

1½ cups (185 g) all-purpose flour

1 teaspoon baking soda

¾ teaspoon coarse salt

½ cup (120 g) vegetable shortening or unsalted butter, or ¼ cup (60 g) of each, at room temperature

¾ cup (175 g) creamy peanut butter

⅔ cup (130 g) granulated sugar, divided

⅓ cup (70 g) packed dark brown sugar

1 large egg

2 tablespoons milk

48 Hershey's milk chocolate kisses, unwrapped

1. Preheat the oven to 375°F (190°C) and line two large baking sheets with baking parchment.

2. In a large bowl, whisk together the flour, baking soda, and salt. In another bowl, with an electric mixer, beat the shortening and peanut butter until well blended. Add ⅓ cup (65 g) of the granulated sugar and all of the brown sugar and beat until fluffy. Beat in the egg and milk. With the mixer on low speed, gradually add the flour mixture until incorporated.

3. Place the remaining ⅓ cup (65 g) granulated sugar in a shallow bowl. Shape the dough into ¾-inch (2 cm) balls and roll in the sugar to coat completely. Transfer to the sheets, spacing 1½ inches (4 cm) apart. Bake until lightly browned, about 10 minutes, rotating the sheets halfway through. Press a chocolate kiss in the center of each cookie. Transfer the sheets to wire racks and let the cookies cool for 5 minutes before transferring directly to the racks to cool completely.

CHOCOLATE HEART THUMBPRINTS

MAKES: ABOUT 36

PREP: 15 MINS

CHILL: 0 MINS

COOK: 15 MINS

A tender yet rich little cookie for Valentine's Day or any other sweet occasion. The dough is mixed by hand, but you can use a mixer.

INGREDIENTS

For the dough :

½ cup (115 g) unsalted butter, at room temperature

½ cup (110 g) packed brown sugar

¾ teaspoon coarse salt

1½ teaspoons vanilla extract

2 tablespoons whole milk

1½ cups (185 g) all-purpose flour

For the filling :

1 tablespoon unsalted butter, at room temperature

2 tablespoons light corn syrup or golden syrup

1 tablespoon water

½ teaspoon vanilla extract

4 ounces (115 g) semisweet chocolate, melted

1. Preheat the oven to 325°F (160°C) and line two large baking sheets with baking parchment.

2. Make the dough: In a large bowl, beat the butter and sugar together until pale and fluffy. Add the salt, vanilla, and milk and beat until incorporated. Fold in the flour. The dough will be soft.

3. Roll the dough into 36 balls. Place the balls on the sheets, spacing 1½ inches (4 cm) apart. Using your thumb, press two indentations in the center of each ball to create a V shape.

4. Bake until the cookies are lightly golden, about 15 minutes, rotating the sheets halfway through. Transfer the sheets to wire racks and let the cookies cool completely.

5. Make the filling: In a small bowl, beat the butter, corn syrup, water, vanilla, and chocolate until smooth. With a pastry bag or tiny spoon, fill each cookie with 1 teaspoon of the chocolate mixture. Let set completely.

YO YOS WITH BERRY BUTTERCREAM

MAKES: ABOUT 25
PREP: 13 MINS
CHILL: 0 MINS
COOK: 15 MINS

The recipe for these Australian cookies is adapted from one by baking teacher and cookbook author Nick Malgieri. You can fill them with any of the buttercreams on page 95.

INGREDIENTS

For the dough :

1½ cups (185 g) all-purpose flour

⅓ cup (40 g) cornstarch

½ teaspoon baking powder

½ teaspoon coarse salt

¾ cup (170 g) unsalted butter, at room temperature

⅔ cup (80 g) confectioners' sugar

1½ teaspoons vanilla extract

For the filling :

Berry Buttercream (page 95)

1. Preheat the oven to 350°F (180°C) and line two large baking sheets with baking parchment.

2. In a large bowl, whisk together the flour, cornstarch, baking powder, and salt. In another bowl, with an electric mixer, beat the butter and sugar until creamy and pale. Beat in the vanilla. With the mixer on low speed, beat in the flour mixture until just incorporated.

3. Using a teaspoon, scoop the dough and roll into balls. Transfer the balls to the sheets, spacing 1½ inches (4 cm) apart. With a lightly floured fork, press the top of each ball lightly to form a crosshatch pattern. (Avoid flattening them too much.)

4. Bake until the cookies are light golden, about 15 minutes, rotating the sheets halfway through. Transfer the sheets to wire racks and let the cookies cool for 3 minutes before transferring directly to the racks. Once cool, sandwich the cookies with the buttercream filling.

FOUR WAYS: BUTTERCREAM

Use any of the following to frost, fill,
and sandwich cookies—from crisp wafers
to cakey rounds, and everything in between.

VANILLA

In a bowl, with an electric mixer, beat
½ cup (115 g) soft unsalted butter until
creamy. Gradually mix in 2 cups (240 g)
sifted confectioners' sugar, followed
by 1 teaspoon vanilla extract and
⅛ teaspoon coarse salt. Add about
2 tablespoons milk and beat until fluffy.
Makes : About 1½ cups (340 g)
Prep : 7 mins

SALTED CHOCOLATE

Melt 3 ounces (85 g) chocolate and
cool for 5 minutes. In a bowl with an
electric mixer, beat ½ cup (115 g) soft
butter until creamy. Gradually mix in
1⅓ cups (200 g) sifted confectioners'
sugar, ½ teaspoon vanilla extract,
¼ teaspoon coarse salt, and the melted
chocolate. Beat in 1 to 2 tablespoons milk
until fluffy.
Makes : About 1½ cups (340 g)
Prep : 7 mins

BROWN SUGAR

Bring ½ cup (115 g) unsalted butter
to a boil in a small pan. Reduce the heat
to medium-low and cook, swirling the
pan, until the butter smells nutty. Transfer
to a heatproof bowl and cool completely.
With an electric mixer, beat the butter until
creamy. Add ½ cup (110 g) dark brown
sugar and beat for 3 minutes. Beat in
¾ cup (90 g) sifted confectioners' sugar
and 1 teaspoon vanilla extract until fluffy.
Beat in 2 tablespoons milk until fluffy.
Makes : About 1½ cups (340 g)
Prep : 7 mins

BERRY

Blitz ¾ cup (100 g) freeze-dried berries
in a blender. In a bowl, beat ½ cup
(115 g) unsalted butter until creamy.
Gradually mix in 1¼ cups (150 g) sifted
confectioners' sugar, 1 teaspoon vanilla
extract, and ½ teaspoon coarse salt.
Add the ground berries gradually until
you reach the desired color. Beat in 3 to
4 tablespoons heavy cream until fluffy.
Makes : About 1½ cups (340 g)
Prep : 7 mins

ALFAJORES

MAKES: ABOUT 20

PREP: 10 MINS

CHILL: 0 MINS

BAKE: 12 MINS

These tiny South American sandwich cookies are filled with dulce de leche, which you can make yourself, or more easily, find at supermarkets and specialty grocers.

INGREDIENTS

¾ cup plus 1 tablespoon (110 g) all-purpose flour, plus extra for dusting

⅓ cup (35 g) cornstarch

¼ teaspoon baking powder

¼ teaspoon coarse salt

⅓ cup (75 g) unsalted butter, at room temperature

¼ cup (50 g) granulated sugar

2 large egg yolks

1 tablespoon brandy

½ teaspoon vanilla extract

Dulce de leche, for filling

Confectioners' sugar, for dusting

1. Preheat the oven to 350°F (180°C) and line two large baking sheets with baking parchment.

2. In a large bowl, whisk together the flour, cornstarch, baking powder, and salt. In another bowl, with an electric mixer, beat the butter and sugar until pale and fluffy. Add the egg yolks, brandy, and vanilla and beat until smooth. With the mixer on low speed, add the flour mixture and beat until just incorporated.

3. Turn the dough out onto a lightly floured counter and pat into a thick round. Using a lightly floured rolling pin, roll the dough out ⅓-inch (8 mm) thick. Using a 1½-inch (4 cm) cutter, cut out rounds. Transfer the rounds to the sheets, spacing ½ inch (1 cm) apart.

4. Bake until the rounds are pale brown on the edges, about 12 minutes, rotating the sheets halfway through. Transfer to a wire rack to cool completely. Once cool, spread a dab of dulce de leche onto half the cookies and sandwich with the other halves. Dust with confectioners' sugar just before serving.

OATMEAL LACE-CHOCOLATE SANDWICHES

MAKES: ABOUT 24

PREP: 10 MINS

CHILL: 0 MINS

BAKE: 10 MINS

INGREDIENTS

1 cup (90 g) old-fashioned rolled oats

1 cup (200 g) sugar

½ cup (115 g) unsalted butter, melted and cooled slightly

½ teaspoon coarse salt

1 large egg

2 teaspoons vanilla extract

4 ounces (115 g) bittersweet chocolate, melted and cooled, for sandwiching

Though these old-fashioned cookies may sound delicate, they are quite sturdy, particularly when sandwiched with melted dark (or milk, semisweet or white) chocolate.

1. Preheat the oven to 350°F (180°C) and line two large baking sheets with baking parchment.

2. Pulse the oats in a food processor until finely chopped (do not grind). Place the sugar in a large bowl, then stir in the butter just until smooth, followed by the oats, salt, egg, and vanilla. Using a ½-teaspoon measure, drop the batter onto the sheets, spacing 3 inches (7.5 cm) apart.

3. Bake until the cookies are brown around the edges, 8 to 10 minutes, rotating the sheets halfway through. Transfer the baking parchment to wire racks and let the cookies cool.

4. Once cool, spread a thin layer of melted chocolate onto the flat sides of half the cookies, then sandwich with the remaining cookies, flat sides down.

ALMOND MACAROONS WITH JAM

MAKES: ABOUT 30

PREP: 10 MINS

CHILL: 0 MINS

COOK: 18 MINS

Not only are these thumbprint cookies a cinch to make—they're also gluten-free. Fill with your favorite jam, Lemon Curd (page 173), or melted chocolate.

INGREDIENTS

3 cups (240 g) sliced blanched almonds

⅔ cup (130 g) sugar

½ teaspoon coarse salt

2 large egg whites

1 teaspoon vanilla extract

½ cup (145 g) jam of your choice, melted

1. Preheat the oven to 350°F (180°C) and line two large baking sheets with baking parchment.

2. Blitz the almonds, sugar, and salt in a food processor just until the nuts are finely ground. Add the egg whites and vanilla and pulse just until the dough forms a ball.

3. With wet hands (the dough is sticky), roll level tablespoons of dough into balls and transfer them to the sheets, spacing 1½ inches (4 cm) apart. Flatten each slightly, then with your thumb, press the center to make an indentation.

4. Bake until the cookies are lightly golden, about 18 minutes, rotating the sheets halfway through. Transfer the sheets to wire racks and let the macaroons cool for 5 minutes before transferring directly to the racks.

5. Using a small spoon, fill each cookie with a little melted jam. Let set before serving.

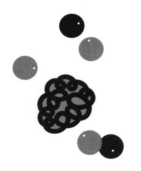

PINEAPPLE PISTACHIO THUMBPRINTS

MAKES: ABOUT 42

PREP: 15 MINS

CHILL: 1 HR

BAKE: 18 MINS

Inspired by Taiwanese pineapple cakes and a pistachio thumbprint from a long-gone bakery in Brooklyn, these cookies are distinctly habit-forming.

INGREDIENTS

1⅔ cups (240 g) shelled pistachios

2¼ cups (280 g) all-purpose flour, plus extra for pressing

½ cup plus 2 tablespoons (130 g) sugar

1 teaspoon baking powder

¼ teaspoon coarse salt

1 cup (225 g) cold unsalted butter, cut into small pieces

2 teaspoons finely grated lime zest

2 large eggs, separated

1½ teaspoons vanilla extract

¾ cup (210 g) pineapple jam, melted, for filling

1. Place 1 cup (135 g) of the pistachios in a food processor with ½ cup (65 g) of the flour and pulse until just finely chopped. Add the remaining 1¾ cups (215 g) flour, the sugar, baking powder, and salt. Add the butter and zest and pulse just a few times. Add the egg yolks and vanilla and pulse until the dough just holds together when squeezed. Chill the dough until firm, at least 1 hour.

2. Preheat the oven to 350°F (180°C) and line two large baking sheets with baking parchment. Finely chop the remaining nuts and place in a shallow bowl. Place the egg whites in another shallow bowl.

3. Form the dough into ¾-inch (2 cm) balls, then roll in the egg whites, followed by the chopped nuts to coat. Place on the sheets, 1½ inches (4 cm) apart. Hold the cookie in place with the thumb and forefinger of one hand, and use the thumb of your other hand to make an indentation in the center of the ball. Using a tiny spoon, fill each indentation with jam. Bake until the cookies are lightly browned, about 18 minutes, rotating the sheets halfway through. Transfer to wire racks to cool.

FILLED AND STUFFED

MAPLE MERINGUE SANDWICHES

MAKES: ABOUT 25
PREP: 15 MINS
CHILL: 0 MINS
BAKE: 1 HR

INGREDIENTS

3 large egg whites,
at room temperature

¼ teaspoon cream
of tartar

Large pinch of coarse salt

¾ cup (150 g) maple sugar

¾ cup (100 g) very finely
chopped walnuts, for
sprinkling and rolling

Maple Whipped Cream
(page 87)

Maple syrup meets freshly fallen snow in
these melt-in-your-mouth cookies. Wait
until just before serving to sandwich the
meringues; otherwise, they will be too soft.

1. Preheat the oven to 225°F (110°C) and line two baking
sheets with baking parchment.

2. With an electric mixer and the whisk attachment, beat
the egg whites, cream of tartar, and salt on low speed
until foamy. Continue whisking while adding the sugar, 1
tablespoon at a time, until the meringue is stiff and glossy.

3. Working in batches, transfer the meringue to a pastry
bag fitted with a ½-inch (1 cm) plain tip and pipe 1-inch
(2.5 cm) rounds onto the sheets, spacing 1 inch (2.5 cm)
apart. Sprinkle lightly with some of the nuts.

4. Bake for 1 hour, rotating the sheets halfway through.
Turn off the oven, and let the meringues dry for several
hours or up to overnight. Remove from the parchment
and store in airtight containers until ready to serve.

5. Before serving, sandwich pairs of meringues with the
cream (½ teaspoon each). Place the remaining nuts in a
bowl, then roll the outer edges of the cookies in the nuts.

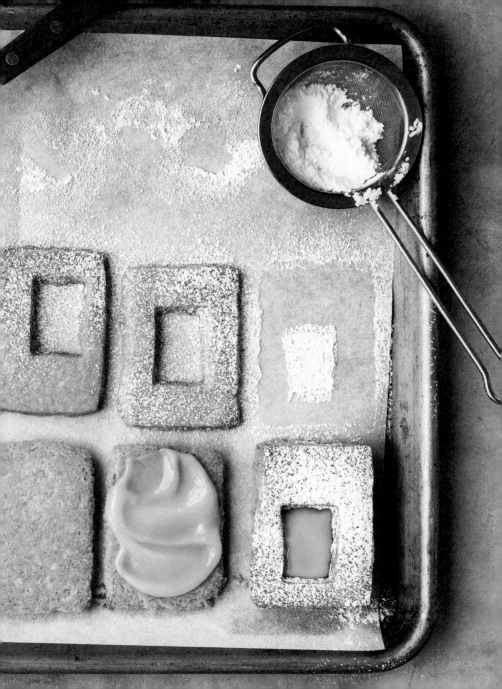

VANILLA BEAN-LEMON CURD SANDWICHES

MAKES: ABOUT 20
PREP: 15 MINS
CHILL: 8 HRS 20 MINS
BAKE: 10 MINS

These tart, sweet treats are right at home on any tea tray. The dough benefits from an overnight rest in the refrigerator; wait until just before serving to dust and fill them.

INGREDIENTS

2¼ cups (290 g) all-purpose flour, plus extra for dusting

½ cup (100 g) superfine or granulated sugar

Large pinch of coarse salt

1 vanilla bean, split lengthwise, seeds scraped, and bean reserved for another use (or 1 tablespoon paste)

1 cup (225 g) cold unsalted butter, cut into cubes

2 large egg yolks

Confectioners' sugar, for dusting

Lemon Curd (page 173), for filling

1. Place the flour, sugar, salt, and vanilla seeds in a food processor and pulse a couple of times just to combine. Add the butter and yolks and pulse until the mixture just comes together when squeezed; do not overwork.

2. On a lightly floured counter, divide the dough in half. Form each half into a thick disk and wrap well in plastic wrap. Chill overnight.

3. Line two large baking sheets with baking parchment. Let the dough rest at room temperature for 10 minutes. On a lightly floured counter, roll out one disk of dough to ¼-inch (5 mm) thick and cut out 3-inch (7.5 cm) rounds, squares, or rectangles with a lightly floured cutter. With a smaller cutter, cut out the centers of half the cookies. Transfer to the sheets, spacing 1½ inches (4 cm) apart; chill for 20 minutes.

4. Preheat the oven to 375°F (190°C). Bake until the cookies are pale golden, 10 minutes, rotating halfway through. Repeat with remaining dough. Transfer the cookies to wire racks to cool. To serve, dust the cutout cookies with confectioners' sugar. Spread the flat sides of the whole cookies with curd and top with the dusted ones.

FILLED AND STUFFED

BACI DI DAMA

MAKES : ABOUT 22
PREP : 15 MINS
CHILL : 3 HRS 20 MINS
BAKE : 15 MINS

The name of these sweet Italian sandwich cookies translates to "Lady's kisses." Flavored with ground nuts, they are filled with melted dark chocolate or, in a pinch, Nutella.

INGREDIENTS

⅔ cup (100 g) blanched almonds

¾ cup (95 g) all-purpose flour

7 tablespoons (100 g) cold unsalted butter, cut into small cubes

Scant ½ cup (85 g) sugar

⅛ teaspoon coarse salt

Melted dark chocolate or chocolate hazelnut spread, for sandwiching

1. Blitz the almonds with 3 tablespoons of the flour in a food processor until finely ground. Add the butter, sugar, salt, and remaining flour and pulse just until the dough starts to come together when squeezed. Transfer to a counter and smear portions of dough with the palm of your hand a few times to help bring it together. Flatten into a thick disk and wrap in plastic wrap. Chill until firm, at least 3 hours.

2. Roll level teaspoons of dough into balls, squeezing tightly to compact them. Place on a large plate or tray and chill for at least 20 minutes.

3. Preheat the oven to 300°F (150°C) and line two large baking sheets with baking parchment.

4. Transfer the dough balls to the sheets, spacing about 1 inch (2.5 cm) apart. Bake until barely golden and very light on the bottom, 15 minutes, rotating the sheets halfway through. Transfer the sheets to wire racks and let the cookies cool completely (they will firm up as they cool). Sandwich pairs of cookies with ½ teaspoon melted chocolate or spread.

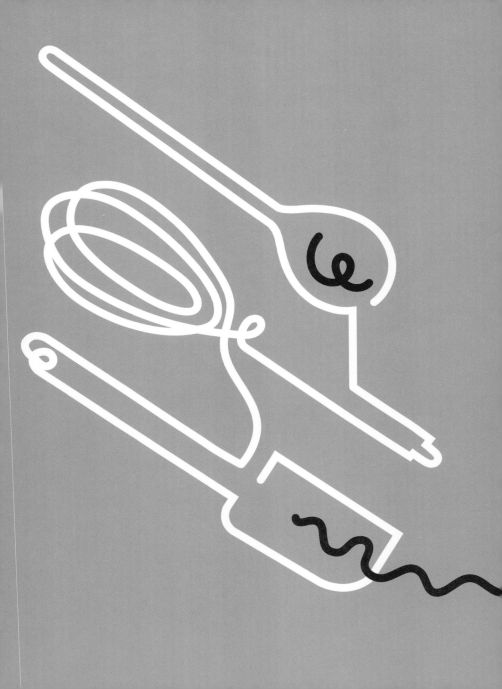

ICED AND GLAZED

ICED SUGAR COOKIES

MAKES: 24 TO 60

PREP: 20 MINS

CHILL: 1¼ HRS

BAKE: 10 TO 18 MINS

INGREDIENTS

3¾ cups (470 g) all-purpose flour, plus extra for dusting

1 teaspoon baking powder

½ teaspoon coarse salt

1 cup (225 g) unsalted butter, at room temperature

1¾ cups (350 g) sugar

2 large eggs

1 teaspoon vanilla extract

Royal Icing, for decorating (optional; page 117)

Sprinkles, sanding sugar, nonpareils, or crumbled freeze-dried fruit, for decorating (optional)

Of the hundreds of recipes for rolled and cut cookies, none is as reliable as this one, adapted from a Martha Stewart recipe. Chilling the cutouts keeps the edges crisp.

1. In a bowl, whisk the flour, baking powder, and salt. In another bowl, with an electric mixer, beat the butter and sugar until pale and fluffy. Add the eggs one at a time, beating well, then mix in the vanilla. With the mixer on low, gradually add the flour mixture, beating until just incorporated. Halve the dough and wrap each piece in plastic wrap. Flatten into disks and chill, at least 1 hour.

2. Preheat the oven to 325°F (160°C) and line two large baking sheets with baking parchment. Let one disk of dough stand at room temperature until soft enough to roll, 10 minutes. On a lightly floured counter, roll out the dough to ¼ inch (5 mm) thickness. With lightly floured cutters, cut out shapes. Transfer the shapes to the sheets and chill until firm, 15 minutes. Roll and cut out scraps.

3. Bake until the cookie edges turn golden, 10 minutes for small cookies, 15 to 18 for large ones. Transfer to wire racks and let the cookies cool. Repeat the process with the second disk of dough. Decorate the cookies with royal icing and toppings, if using. Let dry completely.

ROYAL ICING

MAKES : ABOUT 1 CUP (225 G)

PREP : 10 MINS

CHILL : 0 MINS

BAKE : 0 MINS

The classic embellishment for cutout cookies of all shapes and sizes, royal icing goes on smooth, takes well to colors of any shade, and dries to a clean finish.

INGREDIENTS

2 large egg whites, preferably organic

3 cups (360 g) sifted confectioners' sugar

Water, as needed

Gel-paste food coloring (optional)

1. With an electric mixer and the whisk attachment, beat the egg whites until foamy. Gradually add the sugar, about ½ cup (60 g) at a time, and beat on medium-high speed until the icing is very thick and holds a stiff peak, about 5 minutes. Add enough water, 1 tablespoon at a time, until the icing no longer holds a peak and is thin enough for piping.

2. If desired, divide the icing into small bowls and tint with food coloring (leave some untinted in case you need to tone other colors down). Use immediately, or cover the surface with plastic wrap and store in an airtight container until ready to decorate cookies.

3. To pipe royal icing, fit a pastry bag with a plastic coupler and a metal piping tip. Place the bag in a tall glass as you fill it a little more than halfway with the icing. Use a small round tip to pipe details directly onto your cooled cookies (page 120). To cover a cookie's surface with icing (pages 2 and 114), start by piping the outline with a small round tip, then switch to a slightly larger round tip and pipe thicker lines from side to side. You don't have to fill in the outline; instead, use a toothpick to extend the lines of wet icing over any uncovered areas. Pop any tiny bubbles on the surface with a toothpick while the icing is still wet, then top with sprinkles or other decorations, if using. Let the icing dry completely before serving.

STAINED GLASS COOKIES

MAKES : ABOUT 50

PREP : 10 MINS

CHILL : 30 MINS

BAKE : 13 MINS

Here's a kid-friendly baking project that can be adapted for any holiday. You'll be delighted at the range of colors you can get with just one bag of assorted hard candies.

INGREDIENTS

Hard candies such as Jolly Ranchers or sour balls, in a variety of colors (about 1 cup (220 g) per color)

Iced Sugar Cookies Dough (page 115)

All-purpose flour, for dusting

1. Preheat the oven to 350°F (180°C) and line two large baking sheets with baking parchment. Place the candies (separated by color) into sealed plastic bags. With a mallet, crush them into very small pieces.

2. Working with one disk of dough at a time, roll out the dough between floured baking parchment to ⅛ inch (3 mm) thickness. Chill until firm, about 30 minutes.

3. With a 2½- or 3-inch (6 or 7.5 cm) square cutter, cut out the dough. Place the squares on the sheets, spacing 1 inch (2.5 cm) apart. Using a tiny star (or other shape) cutter, cut out the center of each square. Bake until the cookies are pale but set, 8 to 10 minutes. Remove the sheets from the oven and fill the cutouts with crushed candy, working quickly but carefully. Bake until the candy is melted and the cookies are golden on the edges, 3 minutes. Transfer the sheets to wire racks and let the cookies cool completely. Make more cookies with the remaining dough and candies.

ICED AND GLAZED

GINGERBREAD COOKIES

MAKES: 36 TO 48
PREP: 15 MINS
CHILL: 2 HRS
BAKE: 15 MINS

What takes a gingerbread cookie from ordinary to extraordinary? The addition of some finely grated citrus zest—in this case, both lemon and orange—and fresh ginger.

INGREDIENTS

4 cups (500 g) all-purpose flour, plus extra for dusting

1½ teaspoons baking soda

1½ teaspoons each of ground cinnamon and ginger

1 teaspoon ground allspice

½ teaspoon each of ground cloves and coarse salt

1 cup (225 g) unsalted butter, at room temperature

¾ cup (150 g) granulated sugar

¾ cup (165 g) packed dark brown sugar

1 large egg

1 tablespoon grated ginger

¼ cup (65 g) molasses

Finely grated zest of 1 lemon and 1 orange

Royal Icing (page 117), for decorating

1. In a bowl, whisk the flour, baking soda, spices, and salt. In another bowl, with an electric mixer, beat the butter with both sugars until fluffy. Beat in the egg, followed by the grated ginger, molasses, and zests. With the mixer on low, gradually add the flour mixture, beating until well combined. Divide the dough in half and wrap each in plastic wrap, flattening into disks. Chill until firm, 2 hours.

2. Preheat the oven to 350°F (180°C) and line two baking sheets with baking parchment. On a lightly floured counter, roll one disk of dough to a ¼ inch (5 mm) thickness. With cutters, cut out shapes as close together as possible. Place on the sheets, spacing 1 inch (2.5 cm) apart. Bake until firm 10 to 15 minutes (depending on the size), rotating the sheets halfway through. Transfer the cookies to wire racks to cool completely. Repeat the process with the remaining disk of dough. Decorate the cooled cookies with royal icing.

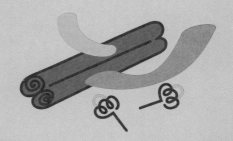

CHOCOLATE CUTOUTS

MAKES : 36 TO 48

PREP : 15 MINS

CHILL : 1 HR

BAKE : 15 MINS

A bowl of melted chocolate is all you need to finish these cookies, though they go well with Royal Icing (page 117) for special occasions.

INGREDIENTS

1½ cups (190 g) cups all-purpose flour, plus extra for dusting

¾ cup (65 g) unsweetened cocoa powder

¼ teaspoon coarse salt

¾ cup (170 g) unsalted butter, at room temperature

1 cup (200 g) sugar

1 large egg

Melted chocolate, for dipping

1. In a bowl, whisk together the flour, cocoa, and salt. In another bowl, with an electric mixer, beat the butter and sugar until pale and fluffy. Beat in the egg. With the mixer on low, gradually beat in the flour mixture. Divide the dough in half and wrap each in plastic wrap, flattening into disks. Chill until firm, at least 1 hour.

2. Preheat the oven to 350°F (180°C) and line baking sheets with baking parchment. Let one disk of dough sit at room temperature for 10 minutes. On a lightly floured counter, roll out the dough to a ¼ inch (5 mm) thickness. With lightly floured cutters, cutout shapes as close to each other as possible. Transfer the cutouts to the sheets, spacing 1 inch (2.5 cm) apart. (If the dough seems soft, chill the cutouts for 10 minutes.) Brush off excess flour.

3. Bake until the cookies are firm, 10 to 15 minutes, depending on the size. Transfer the cookies to wire racks to cool completely. Repeat the process with the remaining dough. Dip the edges of the cooled cookies in melted chocolate, or decorate as desired.

ICED AND GLAZED

RICOTTA COOKIES

MAKES : ABOUT 36

PREP : 15 MINS

CHILL : 0 MINS

BAKE : 18 MINS

No Italian-American cookie tray is complete without a dozen or so of these cakey, lemony cookies. For the best flavor and texture, make sure to use whole-milk ricotta.

INGREDIENTS

2¼ cups (280 g) all-purpose flour

1 teaspoon baking powder

¼ teaspoon coarse salt, plus a pinch

½ cup (115 g) unsalted butter, at room temperature

¾ cup plus 2 tablespoons (180 g) granulated sugar

2 large eggs

1 cup (225 g) ricotta

Finely grated zest of 1 lemon, plus 2 to 3 tablespoons fresh juice

1½ teaspoons vanilla extract

2 cups (240 g) confectioners' sugar

Sprinkles, for decorating

1. Preheat the oven to 325°F (160°C) and line two large baking sheets with baking parchment.

2. In a bowl, whisk the flour, baking powder, and ¼ teaspoon salt. In another bowl, with an electric mixer, beat the butter and granulated sugar until light and fluffy. Add the eggs, one at a time, beating well, then the ricotta, zest, and vanilla. With the mixer on low, gradually add the flour mixture and beat until just incorporated.

3. Form level tablespoons of the dough into balls (if the dough is too sticky, wet your hands lightly) and place on the sheets, spacing 2 inches (5 cm) apart. Bake until the cookies are puffed, and the bottoms are golden brown, 15 to 18 minutes, rotating the sheets halfway through. Transfer the cookies to wire racks to cool completely.

4. In a bowl, whisk the lemon juice, confectioners' sugar, and pinch of salt. Add more juice or sugar as needed, to adjust the thickness. Dip the top of each cookie in the glaze then invert and scatter sprinkles over the tops. Let dry completely before serving.

COCONUT MACAROONS WITH CHOCOLATE GLAZE

MAKES: ABOUT 36
PREP: 15 MINS
CHILL: 0 MINS
BAKE: 20 MINS

INGREDIENTS

4 large egg whites

⅔ cup (130 g) sugar

2 teaspoons vanilla extract

½ teaspoon coarse salt

4¼ cups (320 g) unsweetened dried shredded coconut

5 ounces (160 g) dark or milk chocolate, melted and kept warm

The best cookie recipes are those with few ingredients and a formula so simple that you can commit it to memory after just a few attempts. Case in point: these five-ingredient macaroons with a melted chocolate finish.

1. Preheat the oven to 350°F (180°C) and line two large baking sheets with baking parchment.

2. In a large bowl, whisk together the egg whites, sugar, vanilla, and salt until blended. Mix in the coconut until well combined. Using a tablespoon measure, form tightly packed mounds of the mixture and drop onto the sheets, spacing about 1 inch (2.5 cm) apart.

3. Bake until the macaroons are golden brown, about 20 minutes, rotating the sheets halfway through. Transfer the sheets to wire racks and let the macaroons cool completely. Dip the macaroons in the melted chocolate and let set before serving.

GLAZED LEMON MADELEINES

MAKES: 12

PREP: 15 MINS

CHILL: 1 HR

BAKE: 12 MINS

Madeleines are the stuff of powerful taste memories (as celebrated by the French novelist Marcel Proust). One bite and it's hard to imagine not getting hooked.

INGREDIENTS

For the madeleines :

¾ cup plus 2 tablespoons (120 g) all-purpose flour, plus extra for molds

⅔ cup (130 g) granulated sugar

½ teaspoon baking powder

¼ teaspoon coarse salt

1 tablespoon finely grated lemon zest

2 large eggs

6½ tablespoons unsalted butter, melted and cooled, plus extra for molds

For the glaze :

2 tablespoons confectioners' sugar

⅛ teaspoon coarse salt

1 tablespoon fresh lemon juice, plus extra as needed

2 tablespoons water

1. In a bowl, whisk together the flour, sugar, baking powder, salt, and zest. Add the eggs one at a time, stirring just until combined. Don't overbeat. Fold in the melted butter just until smooth. Cover and chill for at least 1 hour.

2. Preheat the oven to 400°F (200°C) and brush a 12-shell madeleine pan with softened butter (even if it's nonstick). Dust the molds lightly with flour.

3. Transfer the batter to a piping or resealable bag with a ½ inch (1 cm) opening. Pipe the batter evenly into each mold. Bake until the edges are brown and the cakes bounce back when lightly pressed, 10 to 12 minutes.

4. Meanwhile, whisk together all the glaze ingredients in a shallow bowl.

5. Transfer the pan of baked madeleines to a wire rack set over a rimmed baking sheet. Let cool for 2 or 3 minutes, then use an offset spatula to loosen the edges. Dip the madeleines in the glaze, one at a time, turning to coat on all sides. Return the glazed madeleines to the wire rack and let set before serving. Madeleines are best eaten on the same day they are baked.

MAPLE-GLAZED PUMPKIN COOKIES

MAKES : ABOUT 48
PREP : 15 MINS
CHILL : 0 MINS
BAKE : 14 MINS

INGREDIENTS

For the cookies :

2 ¼ cups (280 g) all-purpose flour

¾ teaspoon each of baking powder and baking soda

¾ teaspoon coarse salt

2 teaspoons each of ground cinnamon and ground ginger

¾ teaspoon grated nutmeg

⅛ teaspoon ground cloves

⅛ teaspoon ground allspice

¾ cup (170 g) unsalted butter, at room temperature

1 ½ cups (330 g) packed brown sugar

2 large eggs, at room temperature

½ teaspoon vanilla paste or extract

1 (15-ounce / 425 g) can pumpkin puree

Toasted pepitas, for topping

For the glaze :

Maple Brown Butter Glaze (page 133)

A coffeeshop staple that's easy to recreate at home, these cakey cookies are nicely spiced and finished with a beautiful brown butter-maple icing. The recipe halves easily.

1. Preheat the oven to 350°F (180°C) and line two large baking sheets with baking parchment.

2. In a large bowl, whisk together the flour, baking powder, baking soda, salt, and spices. In another bowl, with an electric mixer, beat the butter and sugar until creamy. Add the eggs, one at a time, beating well after each. Beat in the vanilla and pumpkin until incorporated. With the mixer on low, gradually add the flour mixture.

3. Drop level tablespoons of dough onto the sheets, spacing 1 ½ inches (4 cm) apart.

4. Bake until the cookies are firm and spring back when lightly pressed, 11 to 14 minutes, rotating the sheets halfway through. Transfer to wire racks to cool completely.

5. Spread the glaze over the tops of the cookies, then sprinkle with pepitas. Let the glaze set before serving.

FOUR WAYS: GLAZES

The following glazes help elevate ordinary cookies into something extraordinary in no time flat, with just a few pantry ingredients.

CHOCOLATE GANACHE

Place 4 ounces (115 g) bittersweet chocolate in a small bowl. Heat 2/3 cup (160 ml) heavy cream and 2 teaspoons light corn syrup in a small saucepan until starting to simmer around the edges. Pour over chocolate and let stand for 5 minutes; stir until smooth. Use immediately.
Makes : About 1 cup (225 g)
Prep : 7 mins

CITRUS

In a bowl, whisk 1 cup (120 g) sifted confectioners' sugar, 2 tablespoons citrus juice, 2 teaspoons finely grated citrus zest, and a pinch of coarse salt until thick enough to spread. Taste and adjust the sweetness or tartness, if needed. For a thinner, more pourable glaze, add more juice. Use immediately.
Makes : About 1 cup (225 g)
Prep : 5 mins

SALTED CARAMEL

In a small heavy saucepan, combine 1/2 cup (100 g) plus 3 tablespoons sugar with 3 tablespoons water, stirring to combine. Over medium-high heat, bring the mixture to a boil and cook until it's a dark golden brown, 4 to 5 minutes, swirling the pan and watching very carefully (do not stir). Take the pan off the heat and slowly and carefully pour in 1/4 cup (60 ml) heavy cream (it will bubble up). Add 2 tablespoons cubed cold unsalted butter and stir until combined. Season with a large pinch of coarse salt. Let cool for 5 minutes before using.
Makes : About 3/4 cup (170 g)
Prep : 10 mins

MAPLE BROWN BUTTER

Sift 2 cups (240 g) confectioners' sugar into a large bowl and add a large pinch of coarse salt. Melt 3 tablespoons butter in a small skillet over medium heat. Once it's melted, cook, swirling, until it starts to brown and golden brown solids fall to the bottom of the pan, about 5 minutes. Pour the browned butter into a small heatproof bowl and refrigerate to cool slightly. In the same skillet, melt another 3 tablespoons butter (don't let it brown), then combine with the browned butter. Pour the butter mixture and 6 tablespoons maple syrup into the bowl with the sugar and whisk until smooth. Use immediately.
Makes : About 1 1/2 cups (360 g)
Prep : 15 mins

GLAZED MASA HARINA COOKIES

MAKES : ABOUT 24
PREP : 45 MINS
REST : 30 MINS
BAKE : 18 MINS

INGREDIENTS

For the cookies :

2 cups (240 g) masa harina (corn flour)

1 cup (200 g) granulated sugar

2 teaspoons ground cinnamon

½ cup (120 g) vegetable shortening or lard, at room temperature

1 large egg, at room temperature

1 teaspoon vanilla extract

¼ cup (60 ml) orange juice or coffee, at room temperature

For the glaze :

1½ cups (180 g) sifted confectioners' sugar

2 tablespoons orange juice, plus extra as needed

1 tablespoon unsalted butter, melted

Pinch of coarse salt

Based on a traditional Mexican pastry, the corn flour cookies can be left unadorned, but a bright citrusy glaze ups the festive factor.

1. In a bowl, whisk the corn flour, sugar, and cinnamon. With an electric mixer, beat in the shortening, egg, vanilla, and ¼ cup (60 ml) juice until a dough comes together. If it is too crumbly to hold together, add a little more liquid until it does. It is not a super moist dough but you should be able to roll it into balls. Let the dough rest at room temperature to hydrate for 30 minutes.

2. Meanwhile, preheat oven to 350°F (180°C) and line two large baking sheets with baking parchment.

3. Roll the dough into 1½-inch (4 cm) balls and transfer to the sheets. Using a shell-shaped cookie stamp (or the bottom of a glass), flatten the cookies. Bake until the bottoms are light golden brown, 15 to 18 minutes, rotating the sheets halfway through. Transfer the cookies to a wire rack to cool.

4. To make the glaze, whisk the confectioners' sugar, 2 tablespoons orange juice, melted butter, and salt in a bowl. If it's too thick, slowly add more juice, 1 teaspoon at a time, until the glaze is the consistency of syrup. Dip the top of each cookie in glaze; let set for 30 minutes before serving.

BIRTHDAY CAKE COOKIES

MAKES : ABOUT 28
PREP : 15 MINS
CHILL : 0 MINS
BAKE : 12 MINS

As an alternative to one large, frosted cake, single-serving, cake-like cookies offer festive fun for everyone. Ice them with any of the buttercreams on page 95.

INGREDIENTS

2¾ cups (340 g) all-purpose flour

½ teaspoon baking soda

½ teaspoon baking powder

¾ teaspoon coarse salt

½ cup (115 g) unsalted butter, at room temperature

1¼ cups (250 g) sugar

2 large eggs, at room temperature

1½ teaspoons vanilla extract

¼ teaspoon almond extract (optional)

1 cup (225 g) sour cream, at room temperature

For the topping :

Buttercream (page 95)

Sprinkles

1. Preheat the oven to 350°F (180°C) and line two large baking sheets with baking parchment.

2. In a large bowl, whisk together the flour, baking soda, baking powder, and salt. In another bowl, with an electric mixer, beat the butter and sugar together until pale and fluffy. Add the eggs, one at a time, and then the extracts, beating well. With the mixer on low, add the flour mixture, alternating with the sour cream, beginning and ending with the flour. Mix until just incorporated.

3. Using a two-tablespoon scoop, drop mounds of dough onto the sheets, spacing 1½ inches (4 cm) apart. Bake until the cookies spring back when lightly pressed, about 12 minutes, rotating the sheets halfway through. Transfer the sheets to a wire rack and let the cookies cool for 5 minutes before transferring them to racks to cool.

4. Frost each cookie with buttercream and top with sprinkles, as desired.

SABLES DRIZZLED WITH CARAMEL

MAKES : ABOUT 28
PREP : 15 MINS
CHILL : 4 HRS
BAKE : 13 MINS

If you'd rather skip the caramel (though you really shouldn't), you can roll the logs in raw or sparkly sanding sugar before slicing and baking.

INGREDIENTS

½ cup (115 g) salted butter

¾ cup plus 2 tablespoons (120 g) all-purpose flour

2 tablespoons cornstarch

¼ teaspoon coarse salt

⅓ cup (65 g) sugar

1 large egg

¾ teaspoon vanilla extract

Salted Caramel Glaze (page 133), for drizzling

Flaky salt, for sprinkling

1. In a small saucepan over medium heat, melt the butter and cook, stirring and swirling the pan occasionally, until it has a nutty fragrance and the flecks on the bottom of the pan turn golden, about 5 minutes. Transfer the butter to a heatproof bowl and chill until firm, about 1 hour.

2. In a bowl, whisk the flour, cornstarch, and salt. In another bowl, with an electric mixer, beat the chilled butter and sugar together until pale and fluffy. Beat in the egg and vanilla until incorporated. With the mixer on low, gradually add the flour mix until just combined.

3. On a large sheet of plastic wrap, form the dough into an 8-inch (20 cm) log, about 1 ½ inches (4 cm) in diameter (you may need to chill it slightly before rolling). Chill, until firm, at least 3 hours.

4. Preheat the oven to 350°F (180°C) and line two large baking sheets with baking parchment. Slice the dough into ¼-inch (5 mm) thick rounds and transfer to the sheets, spacing 1 ½ inches (4 cm) apart. Bake just until the edges are slightly darker than the centers, 10 to 13 minutes. Transfer the sheets to a rack, let the cookies cool for 5 minutes, then transfer the cookies to the rack to cool completely. Top the cookies with caramel and salt.

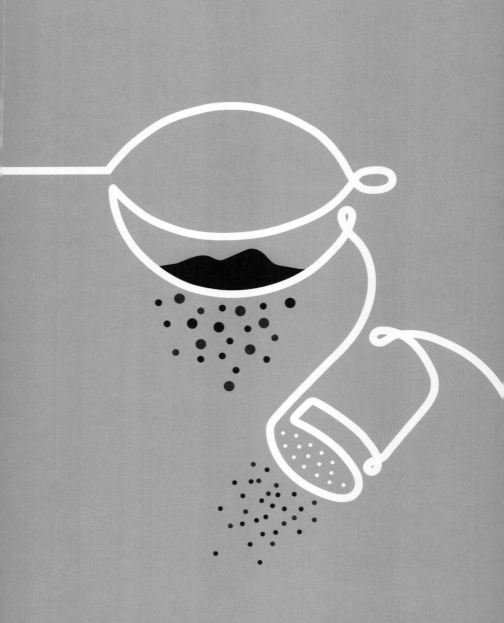

DUSTED AND
SPRINKLED

MOCHA MERINGUE HEARTS

MAKES : ABOUT 30
PREP TIME : 15 MINS
CHILL TIME : 0 MINS
BAKE TIME : 14 MINS

INGREDIENTS

3 large egg whites,
at room temperature

½ cup (100 g) granulated
sugar

½ cup (100 g) Espresso
Sugar (page 151)

¼ teaspoon cream of tartar

Pinch of coarse salt

½ teaspoon vanilla extract

3 ounces (90 g)
unsweetened chocolate,
melted and cooled

Unsweetened cocoa
powder, for dusting

These light and airy gluten-free cookies are easier to make than they look. If you don't have espresso sugar, you can substitute 1 cup (200 g) granulated sugar mixed with 1 teaspoon ground espresso powder for both sugars in the recipe.

1. Preheat the oven to 300°F (150°C) and line two large baking sheets with baking parchment.

2. In a heatproof bowl, whisk together the egg whites, both sugars, cream of tartar, vanilla, and salt. Place the bowl over a pot of simmering water and whisk until the egg whites are warm and the mixture is not grainy.

3. With an electric mixer, whisk the mixture on medium speed until cooled to room temperature (take care not to overbeat; the meringue should be glossy but not dry). Pour the melted chocolate over the meringue and fold it in with a flexible spatula just until the color is even.

4. Transfer the meringue to a large pastry bag fitted with an open star tip. Pipe 2-inch (5 cm) hearts onto the prepared sheets, spacing them 1 to 2 inches (2.5 to 5 cm) apart. Bake until the meringues are set and crisp on the outside but still soft on the insides, 12 to 14 minutes.

5. Transfer the meringues (still on the parchment) to a wire rack to cool completely. Once cool, dust lightly with cocoa powder.

DUSTED AND SPRINKLED

TOASTED PECAN SNOWBALLS

MAKES : ABOUT 48
PREP TIME : 15 MINS
CHILL TIME : 1 HR
BAKE TIME : 30 MINS

These cookies go by many names, including Mexican Wedding Cookies, Noel Nut Balls, and Russian Tea Cakes. No matter what they're called, they are always a big hit.

INGREDIENTS

1 ½ cups (270 g) pecan halves

1 cup (225 g) unsalted butter, at room temperature

¾ cup (150 g) granulated sugar

1 teaspoon vanilla paste or extract

¼ teaspoon almond extract

2 cups plus 2 tablespoons (280 g) all-purpose flour

¼ teaspoon coarse salt

Confectioners' sugar, for coating

1. Preheat the oven to 350°F (180°C) and line two large baking sheets with baking parchment.

2. Toast the pecans on another baking sheet until fragrant and well browned, 12 minutes or a little longer, tossing halfway through. (For the best flavor, they should be just short of burnt.) Let the nuts cool completely before very finely chopping (a few slightly larger pieces are OK).

3. In a large bowl, with an electric mixer, beat the butter, granulated sugar, and both extracts until light and fluffy. With the mixer on low, beat in half the flour and the salt, then beat in the remaining flour and the nuts. Chill the dough for at least 1 hour.

4. Preheat the oven to 350°F (180°C). Roll the dough into ¾-inch (2 cm) balls. Place on the sheets, spacing 1 inch (2.5 cm) apart. Bake until firm, about 15 minutes, rotating the sheets halfway through. Transfer the cookies to a wire rack to cool completely. Toss the cooled cookies in confectioners' sugar to coat. Just before serving, toss them again.

SHORTBREAD WEDGES

MAKES: 12

PREP TIME: 15 MINS

CHILL TIME: 20 MINS

BAKE TIME: 50 MINS

INGREDIENTS

1 cup (225 g) salted butter, at room temperature, plus extra for the pan

2 cups (250 g) all-purpose flour

1 to 2 tablespoons espresso powder, to taste

1 teaspoon coarse salt

¾ cup (90 g) confectioners' sugar

About 2 tablespoons Espresso Sugar (page 151), for sprinkling

Shortbread can be a blank slate for other flavors. Try adding citrus zest in place of the ground espresso in the dough, and lemon sugar (page 151) on top, as an example.

1. Coat a 9-inch (23 cm) fluted tart pan or springform pan with softened butter.

2. In a bowl, whisk the flour, espresso powder, and salt. In another bowl, with an electric mixer on medium speed, beat the butter until creamy. With the mixer on low, gradually add the confectioners' sugar, beating until pale and fluffy. Add the flour mixture and beat until combined.

3. Press the dough into the pan in an even layer and chill until firm, about 20 minutes.

4. Preheat the oven to 300°F (150°C). Using a bench scraper or knife, cut the dough into 12 wedges, then use a wooden skewer to prick the wedges all over.

5. Bake until golden brown and firm, 45 to 50 minutes, rotating the pan halfway through. Transfer the pan to a wire rack and cut along the scored lines. Sprinkle evenly with the flavored sugar. Let the shortbread cool completely in the pan.

ROSEWATER-PISTACHIO MERINGUES

MAKES : ABOUT 48
PREP TIME : 15 MINS
CHILL TIME : 0 MINS
BAKE TIME : 2 HRS

INGREDIENTS

4 large egg whites

¼ teaspoon cream of tartar

1 cup (200 g) superfine or granulated sugar

Large pinch of coarse salt

1 teaspoon rosewater

Very finely chopped pistachios, for sprinkling (about ¼ cup / 35 g)

These cookies are scented with just a trace of rosewater, for a subtly floral and not at all overpowering effect. Finely chopped pistachios add hints of color and crunch.

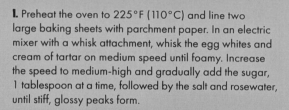

I. Preheat the oven to 225°F (110°C) and line two large baking sheets with parchment paper. In an electric mixer with a whisk attachment, whisk the egg whites and cream of tartar on medium speed until foamy. Increase the speed to medium-high and gradually add the sugar, 1 tablespoon at a time, followed by the salt and rosewater, until stiff, glossy peaks form.

2. Using two large spoons, form the meringue into mounds, spacing about 1 inch (2.5 cm) apart on the prepared sheets. Sprinkle the meringues with pistachios and bake for 30 minutes. Reduce the oven temperature to 200°F (90°C) and bake until the meringues are crisp and bone-dry, another 60 to 90 minutes. Transfer the meringues to a wire rack to cool completely. They are best served the day they are baked, though you can store them in airtight containers for a day or two. Use leftover meringues to make Eton Mess (page 167).

FOUR WAYS: FLAVORED SUGARS

VANILLA

**MAKES : ABOUT 1 CUP
(225 G)**

PREP TIME : 5 MINS

CHILL TIME : 0 MINS

BAKE TIME : 0 MINS

INGREDIENTS

1 cup (200 g) sugar

1 vanilla bean, split lengthwise in half, seeds scraped out

Keep any of these DIY pantry powerhouses on hand as a finish for baked shortbread, or to coat balls of dough before baking.

Place the sugar and vanilla bean seeds in a food processor. Add the halved bean and pulse to a fine powder. Store in an airtight jar until ready to use.

ESPRESSO

Pulse 1 cup (200 g) sugar and 1½ tablespoons espresso powder in a food processor three or four times.

HERB

Finely chop 2 teaspoons fresh herbs, such as mint. Pulse in a food processor with 1 cup (200 g) sugar a few times. Store in an airtight container in the refrigerator.

LEMON

Remove the outer peel of 1 large organic lemon, leaving behind the bitter white pith, and blitz the peel in a food processor with 1 cup (200 g) sugar until combined. Store in an airtight container in the refrigerator.

VANILLA NUT CRESCENTS

MAKES: 54
PREP TIME: 15 MINS
CHILL TIME: 1 HR
BAKE TIME: 18 MINS

With Viennese coffee house vibes, these tender, buttery treats are covered in a thick blanket of vanilla-scented powdered sugar.

INGREDIENTS

1 cup (225 g) unsalted butter, at room temperature

2/3 cup (130 g) granulated sugar

1/4 teaspoon coarse salt

2 teaspoons vanilla paste or extract

1 large egg yolk

2 1/2 cups (310 g) all-purpose flour

1 1/2 cups (200 g) walnuts, finely ground (in a food processor or blender), or very finely chopped by hand

3/4 cup (90 g) confectioners' sugar

2 tablespoons Vanilla Sugar (page 151)

1. With an electric mixer on medium speed, beat the butter, granulated sugar, and salt until light and fluffy. Beat in the vanilla and yolk until combined. With the mixer on low, gradually add the flour. Stir in the nuts. Chill the dough until firm, about 1 hour.

2. Preheat the oven to 325°F (160°C) and line two baking sheets with baking parchment. In a small bowl, combine the confectioners' sugar and vanilla sugar.

3. Divide the dough in half, then divide each half into thirds. Working with one piece at a time (keep the others covered), roll into a 1-inch (2.5 cm) log about 9 inches (23 cm) long. Cut into nine 1-inch (2.5 cm) pieces, and roll each about 3 inches (7.5 cm) long, thicker in the middle and tapered on the ends. Transfer to the sheets, spacing 1 inch (2.5 cm) apart, and bend each slightly to form a wide C shape.

4. Bake until the cookies are light golden on the ends, 15 to 18 minutes, rotating the sheets halfway through. Let the cookies cool on the sheets for 2 minutes, then carefully transfer them to the racks set over baking parchment. Dust the tops of the cookies generously with the sugar mixture.

BISCOCHITOS

MAKES : ABOUT 48
PREP TIME : 15 MINS
CHILL TIME : 1 HR
BAKE TIME : 15 MINS

This recipe is adapted from one by the tourism board of New Mexico, where it's the official state cookie. Traditional recipes include lard, but this one uses butter and shortening.

INGREDIENTS

3 cups (375 g) all-purpose flour

1 tablespoon anise seeds, lightly toasted and crushed

1 ½ teaspoons baking powder

½ teaspoon coarse salt, plus a pinch

½ cup (115 g) unsalted butter, at room temperature

½ cup (115 g) vegetable shortening

½ cup plus 2 teaspoons (110 g) sugar

2 large eggs

2 tablespoons brandy

1 tablespoon ground cinnamon

1. In a bowl, whisk the flour, anise seeds, baking powder, and ½ teaspoon salt. In another bowl, with an electric mixer, beat the butter and shortening until creamy. Add ¼ cup plus 2 teaspoons of the sugar and beat until very light. Beat in the eggs and brandy. On low speed, add the flour mixture and mix until just combined. Halve the dough; place each half between sheets of baking parchment and roll until ¼ inch (5 mm) thick. Chill in the refrigerator or freezer for 30 to 60 minutes.

2. Combine the remaining ¼ cup (50 g) sugar, the cinnamon, and pinch of salt in a bowl. Preheat the oven to 350°F (180°C) and line baking sheets with baking parchment.

3. Using cutters, cut the dough into stars (moons are also traditional) and transfer to the sheets, spacing 1 inch (2.5 cm) apart. Sprinkle with the cinnamon sugar. Bake until the cookies are golden and set, 12 to 15 minutes. Let the cookies cool for a few minutes on the sheets before transferring them to wire racks to cool completely.

FUDGY CRINKLE COOKIES

MAKES: ABOUT 50
PREP TIME: 15 MINS
CHILL TIME: 2 HRS
BAKE TIME: 12 MINS

Crinkle cookies go by other names, including quakes and volcanos, thanks to the way that the chocolate dough appears to erupt through the snow-white powdered sugar.

INGREDIENTS

1¾ cups (215 g) all-purpose flour, plus extra for dusting

1 teaspoon each of baking powder and baking soda

1 cup (88 g) unsweetened cocoa powder

¼ teaspoon coarse salt

½ cup (115 g) unsalted butter, at room temperature

1 cup (220 g) packed dark brown sugar

¾ cup (150 g) granulated sugar, plus ½ cup (100 g) for rolling

4 large eggs

1½ teaspoons vanilla extract

½ cup (60 g) confectioners' sugar

1. In a bowl, whisk together the flour, baking powder, baking soda, cocoa, and salt. In another bowl, with an electric mixer, beat the butter, dark brown sugar, and the ¾ cup (150 g) granulated sugar until light and fluffy. Add the eggs, one at a time, then the vanilla. With the mixer on low, gradually add the flour mix until just incorporated. Chill the dough until firm, 2 hours.

2. Preheat the oven to 350°F (180°C) and line two large baking sheets with baking parchment.

3. Place the ½ cup (100 g) granulated sugar and the confectioners' sugar in two shallow bowls. With lightly floured hands, roll the dough into ¾-inch (2 cm) balls, then roll in granulated sugar followed by confectioners' sugar. Place on the sheets, spacing 1½ inches (4 cm) apart. Bake until set and crackled, about 12 minutes, rotating the sheets halfway through. Transfer the sheets to a wire rack and let the cookies cool for 5 minutes before transferring to the racks to cool completely.

PRETZEL COOKIES

MAKES: 24
PREP TIME: 15 MINS
CHILL TIME: 1 HR 10 MINS
BAKE TIME: 10 MINS

To make this sweet take on the salty snack, a rich chocolate cookie dough is rolled into ropes, twisted into pretzel shapes, and sprinkled with Swedish pearl sugar.

INGREDIENTS

1 cup (125 g) all-purpose flour, plus extra for dusting

3 tablespoons unsweetened cocoa powder

¼ teaspoon instant espresso powder

Large pinch of coarse salt

½ cup (115 g) unsalted butter, at room temperature

⅔ cup (130 g) granulated sugar

1 large egg plus 1 large egg white, for brushing

½ teaspoon vanilla extract

Swedish pearl sugar, for sprinkling

1. In a bowl, whisk the flour, cocoa, espresso powder, and salt. In another bowl, with an electric mixer, beat the butter and sugar on medium speed until light and fluffy. Beat in the whole egg and vanilla until combined. With the mixer on low, gradually add the flour mixture until just combined. Chill the dough until firm, about 1 hour.

2. Roll the dough into 24 even-size balls. Place the balls on a plate and refrigerate or freeze while the oven heats.

3. Preheat the oven to 375°F (190°C) and line two large baking sheets with baking parchment. Lightly beat the remaining egg white in a small bowl.

4. On a lightly floured counter, roll each ball into a 10-inch (25 cm) long rope, then transfer the rope to a sheet and form into a pretzel shape, pressing in the ends to help them adhere. Chill for 10 minutes. Brush off any excess flour.

5. Brush each pretzel with the beaten egg white, then sprinkle generously with pearl sugar. Bake until the pretzels are firm, about 10 minutes, rotating the sheets halfway through. Let the pretzels cool on the sheets for 2 minutes, then transfer them to a wire rack to cool completely.

DUSTED AND SPRINKLED

SUGAR-SPICED GRAHAMS

MAKES : ABOUT 30
PREP TIME : 15 MINS
CHILL TIME : 1 HR 20 MINS
BAKE TIME : 20 MINS

INGREDIENTS

For the cookies :

1 ¼ cups (155 g) all-purpose flour, plus extra for dusting

1 ¼ cups (150 g) whole wheat pastry flour

½ cup (60 g) toasted wheat germ

¾ teaspoon baking soda

¾ teaspoon ground cinnamon

½ teaspoon coarse salt

1 cup (225 g) unsalted butter, at room temperature

¾ cup (165 g) packed brown sugar

2 tablespoons honey

For the topping :

3 tablespoons raw sugar

½ teaspoon each of ground cardamom and cinnamon

⅛ teaspoon each ground nutmeg and black pepper

As cookies go, graham crackers are fairly ordinary. A sparkling combination of raw sugar and warm spices sprinkled on top makes this homemade version extra special.

1. In a bowl, whisk together both flours, wheat germ, baking soda, cinnamon, and salt. In another bowl, with an electric mixer on medium speed, beat the butter and brown sugar until fluffy. Beat in the honey. With the mixer on low, gradually add the flour mixture.

2. Divide the dough in half and shape each half into a rectangle. Wrap in plastic wrap and chill for 20 minutes. On lightly floured baking parchment, roll each piece a little large than a 7½ by 12-inch (19 by 30 cm) rectangle about ¼ inch (5 mm) thick. Using a ruler and pastry wheel, trim the edges and cut out 24 crackers, each 3 by 2½ inches (8 by 6.5 cm), and prick all over with a fork. Chill the dough on the parchment until firm, about 1 hour.

3. Preheat the oven to 350°F (180°C). Meanwhile, combine the topping ingredients in a small bowl.

4. Sprinkle the crackers with the topping, and bake until golden brown, 20 to 24 minutes, rotating the sheets halfway through. Cut the crackers again, separating them. Let them cool completely on the sheets.

CRUMBLED AND STACKED

RASPBERRY-ROSEWATER-PISTACHIO ETON MESS

MAKES: 4
PREP: 15 MINS
CHILL: 0 MINS
BAKE: 0 MINS

INGREDIENTS

1 cup (225 g) heavy cream

¼ cup (55 g) labneh

¼ cup (30 g) confectioners' sugar, sifted

¾ teaspoon vanilla extract

4 cups (480 g) fresh raspberries

8 Rosewater-Pistachio Meringues (page 149)

¼ cup (30 g) finely chopped pistachios

Edible, pesticide-free rose petals, to decorate (optional)

A fine mess, indeed: Crumbled rosewater meringues (page 149), fresh raspberries, chopped pistachios, and labneh-whipped cream make up a slightly sweet, subtly floral, and deliciously ethereal dessert.

1. In a chilled metal bowl, whip the cream, labneh, sugar, and vanilla together until soft peaks form. Fold half of the raspberries into the mixture, smashing them lightly against the side of the bowl, but not fully incorporating them. The cream should be white with streaks of pink.

2. Break the meringues into chunks and divide among four serving bowls. Top with the cream mixture, along with some raspberries. Top with the remaining raspberries, pistachios, and rose petals, if using, just before serving.

S'MORES SUNDAES

SERVES: 2
PREP: 10 MINS
CHILL: 0 MINS
BAKE: 10 MINS

Assembly is everything here: Crumble the crackers, make the fudge sauce, then broil the marshmallows and pile it all together.

INGREDIENTS

For the hot fudge sauce :

¼ cup (60 ml) heavy cream

1 tablespoon unsalted butter

3 tablespoons granulated sugar

3 packed tablespoons dark brown sugar

⅛ teaspoon coarse salt

¼ cup (25 g) sifted unsweetened cocoa powder

For the sundaes :

4 large marshmallows or ⅔ cup (30 g) miniature marshmallows

Vanilla ice cream

4 Sugar-Spiced Grahams (page 163), crumbled into small pieces

1. In a small heavy saucepan over medium heat, stir the cream and butter until the mixture just comes to a boil. Add both sugars and the salt and stir until the mixture is smooth. Reduce the heat to low and whisk in the cocoa until smooth. The sauce will be thick and glossy. Keep warm while you assemble the sundaes. (If not serving the sauce immediately, refrigerate it, then reheat it in a bowl over simmering water.)

2. Line a rimmed baking sheet with foil and preheat the broiler with a rack set 6 inches (15 cm) from the flame. Place the marshmallows atop the foil and broil just until golden brown, watching closely to prevent them burning.

3. In serving bowls, layer crumbled crackers, scoops of ice cream, and drizzles of hot fudge sauce. Top with the marshmallows and serve, with more sauce on the side.

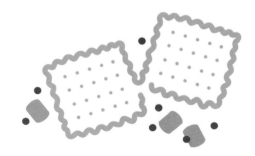

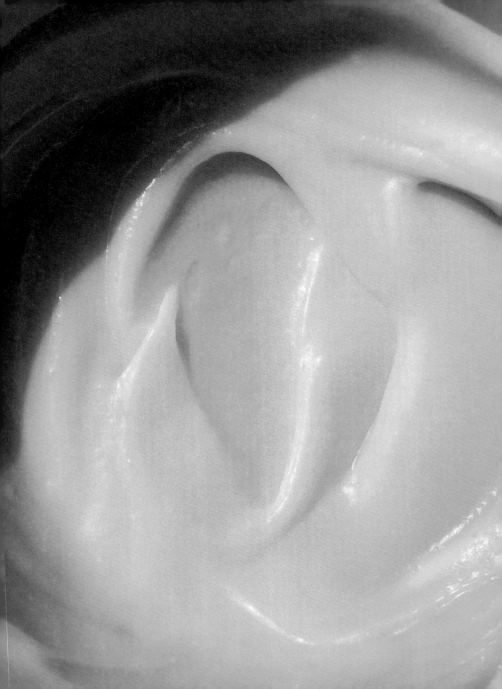

FOUR WAYS: CURD

LEMON

MAKES : 1 CUP (225 G)
PREP : 15 MINS
CHILL : 1 HR
BAKE : 0 MINS

INGREDIENTS

10 tablespoons (125 g) sugar

½ teaspoon coarse salt

1 large egg, plus 3 large yolks

2 teaspoons finely grated lemon zest, plus ⅓ cup (80 ml) fresh juice (from 2 to 3 lemons)

3 tablespoons unsalted butter

If you've never made curd, you're in for a treat. Use it to fill sandwich or thumbprint cookies, or fold it into whipped cream.

1. In a nonreactive pot, whisk together the sugar and salt. Whisk in the whole egg and yolks, followed by the zest and juice. Over medium heat, bring the mixture to a simmer, whisking, until bubbling in the center and thickened. Remove from the heat and whisk in the butter.

2. Strain through a fine-mesh strainer set over a bowl. Press plastic wrap directly on the surface and let cool completely. Refrigerate until thickened and cold, at least 1 hour.

GRAPEFRUIT CURD

Follow the recipe above, substituting grapefruit juice and zest for the lemon.

LIME CURD

Follow the recipe above, substituting lime juice and zest for the lemon.

ORANGE CURD

Follow the recipe above, replacing orange juice and zest for the lemon and reducing the sugar to ½ cup (100 g).

MADELEINE TRIFLES WITH LEMON CREAM

SERVES: 2

PREP: 10

CHILL: 8 HRS

BAKE: 0 MINS

Because madeleines are best eaten the day they're baked, why not make trifle out of the leftovers. You can scale up these proportions to make a larger dessert to serve many.

INGREDIENTS

4 Glazed Lemon Madeleines (page 128)

¼ cup (60 g) Lemon Curd (page 173)

1 cup (240 ml) Vanilla Whipped Cream (page 87), plus extra for topping

Finely grated lemon zest, to decorate

1. With a serrated knife, slice the madeleines into thirds.

2. Gently fold the lemon curd into the whipped cream with a flexible spatula without deflating.

3. In a tall glass or goblet, layer half the cream and half the madeleine slices, beginning with the cream and ending with madeleine. Repeat to make a second trifle with the remaining cream and madeleines. Cover each with plastic wrap and refrigerate for several hours (preferably overnight) to let the madeleines soften. When ready to serve, dollop with whipped cream and decorate with lemon zest.

COOKIES AND CREAM MINI STACK CAKES

MAKES: 2

PREP: 10 MINS

CHILL: 8 HRS

BAKE: 0 MINS

INGREDIENTS

10 Chocolate Wafers
(page 65)

About 1 cup (240 ml)
flavored whipped cream
(page 87)

Chocolate shavings,
to decorate

Made with wafers and whipped cream, zebra cake is among the most beloved, old-school icebox desserts. This riff is scaled down to make individual stacked cakes. Use any of the whipped creams on page 87.

1. Place a chocolate wafer on a plate. Using an offset spatula, spread about 1 tablespoon of whipped cream over the top, then continue to layer four more cookies, with the same amount of whipped cream between each. Top the final cookie with about 2 to 3 tablespoons of cream. Repeat with the remaining five cookies and cream to make another stack cake.

2. Cover the cookies and refrigerate for several hours or preferably overnight. The cookies will soften and become sliceable in that time. Decorate with chocolate shavings.

PEPPERMINT-BARK ICE CREAM SANDWICHES

MAKES: 4

PREP: 15 MINS

CHILL: 12 HRS

BAKE: 0 MINS

INGREDIENTS

1 pint (473 ml) vanilla ice cream

¼ cup (25 g) crushed peppermint candies (candy canes or round mints), plus ½ cup (50 g) extra for rolling

½ teaspoon peppermint extract, or more to taste

8 Chocolate Wafers (page 65)

Inspired by peppermint bark, everyone's favorite holiday treat, the frozen sandwiches are composed of leftover Chocolate Wafers (page 65), crushed candies, peppermint extract, and ice cream.

1. Let the ice cream soften at room temperature for about 10 minutes, then place in the bowl of an electric mixer and beat with the paddle attachment until very soft. Add the ¼ cup (25 g) peppermint candies and the extract and beat just until incorporated. Transfer to an airtight container and freeze until hardened.

2. To assemble the sandwiches, place a scoop of ice cream (about ½ cup / 125 g) on one wafer then cover with another. Repeat to make three more sandwiches. Place the remaining ½ cup (50 g) crushed candies in a shallow bowl and roll the sides in the candies to cover completely. Wrap tightly in plastic wrap and freeze overnight before serving.

BOOZY COOKIE BALLS

MAKES: ABOUT 24

PREP: 20 MINS

CHILL: 8 HRS

BAKE: 0 MINS

INGREDIENTS

1 ¼ cups (300 g)
Chocolate Wafers crumbs
(page 65)

½ cup plus 2 tablespoons
(100 g) toasted walnuts
or pecans

¼ cup (60 ml) whiskey,
bourbon, rum, brandy,
or Scotch whisky

½ cup (60 g)
confectioners' sugar,
plus 1 cup (120 g)
for rolling

2 tablespoons
unsweetened cocoa
powder

1 tablespoon golden
syrup, light corn syrup,
or honey

Pinch of coarse salt

This party favorite makes good use of leftover cookies. Chocolate wafers and vanilla wafers are the classic choices, but you can use gingersnaps, graham crackers, or speculaas in their place, to equally festive effect.

1. Place the cookie crumbs and nuts in a food processor and pulse until finely ground. In a large bowl, stir to combine the liquor, ½ cup (60 g) confectioners' sugar, cocoa powder, syrup, and salt. Add the liquor mixture to the crumb mixture and pulse until just combined. Transfer to a bowl and let stand for several hours at room temperature, or cover and refrigerate overnight.

2. The next day, place the 1 cup (120 g) confectioners' sugar in a shallow bowl. Roll the crumb mixture into small balls, 2 levels teaspoons each, then drop in the bowl of confectioners' sugar and roll until covered completely. The balls can be refrigerated in an airtight container up to three weeks. Roll in confectioners' sugar again before serving, if desired.

YOGURT AND FRUIT WITH CRUMBLED GINGERSNAPS

MAKES : 1

PREP : 5 MINS

CHILL : 0 MINS

BAKE : 0 MINS

INGREDIENTS

2 or 3 Triple-Threat Gingersnaps (page 33), broken into pieces

1 cup (225 g) plain yogurt

1 cup (155 g) cherries, pitted and halved, plus 1 whole cherry to decorate; or other seasonal fruit of your choice, cut into bite-size pieces if large

Just about any leftover cookie can be broken into pieces and layered with yogurt and fresh fruit to make a sweet and simple dessert.

In a small bowl, layer the crumbled gingersnaps, yogurt, and cherries. Decorate with a whole cherry and serve.

SPECULAAS COOKIE BUTTER

MAKES: ABOUT 1 CUP (225 G)

PREP: 5 MINS

CHILL: 0 MINS

BAKE: 0 MINS

INGREDIENTS

5 ¼ ounces (150 g) Speculaas (page 81) (about 10 cookies)

½ cup (120 ml) water

¼ teaspoon ground cinnamon

Large pinch of coarse salt

2 tablespoons golden syrup, honey, or maple syrup

½ cup (115 g) cold unsalted butter or coconut oil

One fun way to use up leftover cookies is to puree them into a "butter." The spread keeps well in the refrigerator, and its uses are many: Dip apple or pear slices in it, drizzle it over ice cream or waffles, or smear it on toast.

Place the Speculaas in a food processor and pulse until finely ground. Add the water, cinnamon, salt, syrup, and butter and process until well blended. Use immediately, or transfer to a storage jar. The butter should keep for several weeks in the refrigerator.

ZABAGLIONE WITH CRUMBLED BISCOTTI

SERVES: 4

PREP: 20 MINS

CHILL: 4 HRS

BAKE: 10 MINS

Biscotti keep well after baking, but after a while you may need a new way to enjoy the cookies. Zabaglione—an Italian custard of egg yolks, sugar, and wine—to the rescue!

INGREDIENTS

4 large egg yolks, preferably organic

¼ cup (50 g) sugar

¼ cup (60 ml) vin santo or dry Marsala wine

¼ teaspoon vanilla extract

6 Cornmeal Fig Biscotti (page 77), crumbled

1. Fill a large saucepan with 1 to 2 inches (2.5 to 5 cm) of water. Bring to a boil, then reduce the heat to a simmer.

2. In a large heatproof bowl, whisk the egg yolks, sugar, and wine until frothy. Set the bowl on top of the pan of water (make sure it's not touching) and whisk vigorously until the mixture is pale and very thick, 5 to 7 minutes. The whisk should leave a trail in the mixture when it is done. Remove the bowl from the heat and whisk in the vanilla extract. Set the bowl over an ice bath and whisk until cool.

3. Spoon the zabaglione into small serving dishes, dividing evenly, and top with the crumbled cookies. Serve immediately.

INDEX

ACKNOWLEDGMENTS

Heartfelt thanks to Susie Theodorou for introducing me to Catie Ziller, who gave me the opportunity to create a book on my favorite subject. Catie led the very talented team who quickly and beautifully pulled it all together: Vivian, Lennart, Michelle, Kathy, and Ainhoa. Thanks to Carla Glasser for her guidance and counsel, to countless friends for their encouragement, and to my family, especially Colin, Nora, and Hugo for their endless support and good cheer as I took over our home kitchen for several months. My longtime colleagues, including many alums of the Martha Stewart Living test kitchen, lent so much to the creation of these recipes. And finally, thanks to Martha herself for instilling in me the incredible value of a well-baked cookie.

Thank you for the lovely loaned table-wear from PropLink and ARJ Los Angeles, https://arj.la/

Hardie Grant North America
2912 Telegraph Ave
Berkeley, CA 94705
hardiegrant.com

Published in the United States by Hardie Grant North America, an imprint of Hardie Grant Publishing Pty Ltd.

Printed in China
FIRST EDITION

Library of Congress Cataloging-in-Publication Data is available upon request
ISBN: 9781964786001
ISBN: (eBook) : 9781964786018

Acquisitions Editor: Catie Ziller
Photographer: Lennart Weibull
Food Stylist: Vivian Lui
Food Stylist Assistant: Ainhoa Hardy
Designer and Illustrator: Michelle Tilly
Copy Editor: Kathy Steer

FSC MIX Paper | Supporting responsible forestry FSC® C020056

NORTH AMERICA

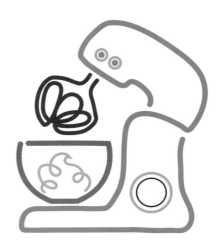